JOURNEY TO THE WEST

A Long March from Eastern Dream to Western Reality

Biao Wang

Copyright © 2023 Biao Wang

All Rights Reserved. No part of this publication may be reproduced, stored in a retrieval system, or transmitted, in any form or by any means, electronic, mechanical, photocopying, recording, or otherwise, without the prior permission of the author.

This book is sold subject to the condition that it shall not, by way of trade or otherwise, be lent, re-sold, hired out or otherwise circulated without the author's prior consent in any form of binding or cover other than that in which it is published and without a similar condition including this condition being imposed on the subsequent purchaser.

Dedicated to my father, who didn't get the chance to see this book come to life.

CONTENTS

Title Page
Copyright
Foreword
Introduction
Author's Note
Map of China
Family Tree

Chapter One: Small Boy, Big Mountains	1
Chapter Two: History	7
Chapter Three: Early Days	22
Chapter Four: Freedom	36
Chapter Five: Off To School	46
Chapter Six: Turbulence	56
Chapter Seven: A Short Break	66
Chapter Eight: Off To The Town	77
Chapter Nine: The West	86
Chapter Ten: Decisions	97
Chapter Eleven: Big, Wide World	106
Chapter Twelve: Working Nine to Five	121

Chapter Thirteen: Off to England	130
Chapter Fourteen: Barry and Bryon	146
Chapter Fifteen: Lightning Bolts	156
Chapter Sixteen: Onwards and Upwards	167
Chapter Seventeen: George Brummell - the World's First Dandy	188
Chapter Eighteen: Learning Curves	200
Chapter Nineteen: My Sister - the 'Iron Queen'	211
Chapter Twenty: Looking Ahead - Now and the Future	224
Acknowledgement	235
About The Author	237

FOREWORD

There's a common adage that says we shouldn't judge a book by its cover. This holds especially true for Biao Wang. On the surface, he may appear as an average man from Leighton Buzzard, a quaint town nestled within the beautiful expanses of Bedfordshire, England. Yet beneath this ordinary facade lies an epic tale that stretches across two vast continents, embodying the very essence of the human spirit and its tenacity.

My introduction to Biao was a lesson in humility. As I stumbled over the pronunciation of his name, he lightheartedly guided me with a memory trick, likening it to the sound of 'meow'. Such a jovial approach to cultural differences encapsulates Biao's character: always making bridges where others might see barriers. Over the years, I've come to cherish this memory, holding it close as a symbol of our deepening friendship.

In the initial three years of our acquaintance, I vividly recall my envy upon learning that Mr. Biao had, at an impressively young age, set up a master tailoring business. This venture enabled him to be among the best-dressed men in Leighton Buzzard and, given Biao's travels, almost anywhere else in the world.

Needless to say, I was, and am still, incredibly impressed by Biao's rise to fame, having come from an extraordinary challenging background in China. He lived his early life in a manner that for most of us would find hard to imagine, and I was most flattered, and our friendship was even more cemented, when he joined the board of my film and television production company a few years ago.

As he most eloquently says "having travelled the world and witnessed many inequalities and the problems such different starting blocks can bring, if I've learned anything, it is that success is always possible, whatever your situation and however your life begins." My key takeaway is this: No matter where you start, success is attainable. His life is a testament to this belief.

Prepare yourself for a riveting journey, filled with trials, triumphs, and invaluable lessons. Biao's story isn't just an autobiography; it's a testament to the resilience of the human spirit and a beacon of inspiration for us all.

Jeffrey Taylor, Los Angeles USA

INTRODUCTION

Biao Wang's memoir 'JOURNEY TO THE WEST' is a fascinating account of the passage of a poor boy from a small, impoverished rural Chinese village to a brilliant, international commercial career and will read as a truly inspiring example of what can be achieved from the least promising background through determination and imagination.

A potted history of modern China leads seamlessly into the story of a young man who, with a combination of remarkable foresight, dedication and courage, has built several successful businesses and established himself at a remarkably young age as a leader in international commercial co-operation.

Here is somebody who has grasped life eagerly, and what his buoyant tale demonstrates is the importance of seeing opportunity and unhesitatingly pursuing it; the story bursts with energy and practical wisdom without any sense of self-importance, whilst taking us stage by stage through Biao's interesting life. From his relatively carefree, if impoverished, childhood in a small village, he takes us, unhurriedly through his education and early struggles, to his great leap forward when he bravely sets out for the unknown world of England, determined to immerse himself in its culture rather than retreating into the comfortable familiarity of his compatriots, seizing opportunities as they arise, always aware of his place in the wider scheme of things.

The narrative offers an intriguing picture of life in contemporary China, and on the way explains much about the Chinese character and culture. His insights into what makes for success are almost incidental as we follow his journey from grinding poverty to commercial achievement. Those from similar backgrounds in any part of the world can take courage from this eloquent account of the power of determination; readers anywhere can share in his infectious enthusiasm for life and all the opportunities it offers.

"JOURNEY TO THE WEST" is also a timely reminder, at a time when the emerging power of China is seen as a threat to the West, that we are all one species, with the same needs and desires, as through his storytelling Biao Wang gives China and the Chinese a human face.

"JOURNEY TO THE WEST" is a cultural bridge as well as a thoroughly enjoyable and absorbing read.

AUTHOR'S NOTE

In Chinese culture and history, the convention of placing the surname before the given name is deeply rooted. This is why, throughout my childhood, even my mother referred to me as Wang Biao. This practice is not merely about sequence but is a manifestation of reverence for our ancestors and the lineage we hail from. It underscores the significance of the family and its role in our individual identities. Staying true to this tradition and to ensure authenticity, all Chinese names mentioned in this book are written with the surname first.

I hope this provides readers with a genuine insight into the Chinese culture and fosters a deeper understanding of the stories and experiences shared herein.

In the book, I refer to my father's father and mother as grandfather and grandmother and to my mother's parents as grandpa and grandma.

MAP OF CHINA

FAMILY TREE

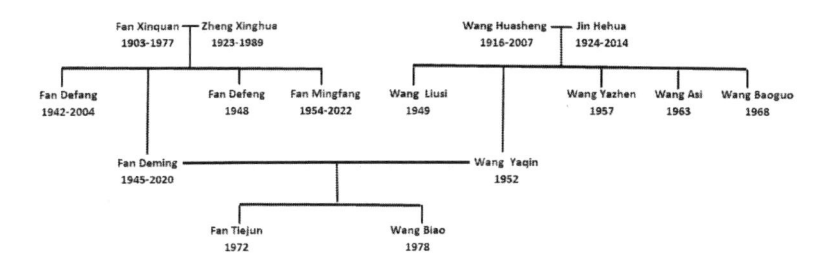

```
Fan Xinquan ── Zheng Xinghua                    Wang Huasheng ── Jin Hehua
 1903-1977       1923-1989                        1916-2007        1924-2014
     │                                                 │
  ┌──┴──┬──────────┬──────────┐          ┌─────────────┼──────────┬──────────┐
Fan Defang   Fan Defeng   Fan Mingfang   Wang Liusi    Wang Yazhen   Wang Asi   Wang Baoguo
1942-2004      1948        1954-2022       1949           1957        1963         1968
     │
Fan Deming ───────────────────────────── Wang Yaqin
1945-2020                                   1952
     │
  ┌──┴────────────┐
Fan Tiejun     Wang Biao
   1972          1978
```

XV

CHAPTER ONE: SMALL BOY, BIG MOUNTAINS

"Your son will have a much better life if he's somewhere else, somewhere far away from the family."

The words of the fortune teller rang out, clear and concise. It can't have been an easy thing to hear – any mother or father wants only the best for their child, after all. They wouldn't have expected my future life satisfaction to be contingent on my being "far away" from them. And not only did she, the fortune teller, state this before my first birthday, but the same prediction was repeated, as I grew older, two or three separate times. In China, the word of fortune tellers is taken incredibly seriously.

Virtually all Chinese babies are taken to have their destinies predicted, and I was no different. My birthday happened to fall on an auspicious day – 20th October 1978 – which in the Lunar Calendar is actually the 19th September, and, as such, was the Goddess of Mercy and Compassion Guan Yin Renunciation Day. Guan Yin is the Chinese name of the Buddhist saint known as

Avalokiteśvara and the Renunciation Day of Guan Yin also falls on the 19th day of the 9th month in the Lunar Calendar. On this day, Guan Yin became a bodhisattva (Buddhist saint). Many people told my parents that this would bring me good fortune and that I was blessed and destined to have a long and happy life.

I'm not a superstitious person and I've been able to formulate my own thoughts so I'm reluctant to rely on something as arbitrary as astrology, the time or date or place of my birth. These are interesting questions, nonetheless – was I born naturally on life's good side? Would fate have smiled on me whatever I decided to do? It may be the case that my personality facilitated a measure of success or perhaps it was the choices my parents made at crucial junctures. But generally, I don't subscribe to the notion of luck. I knew, from my boyhood, that if I wanted to achieve something, I would have to do it myself, with hard work and perseverance.

So was I lucky? As a young boy, I certainly didn't feel it. Born in the village of Fangshuicun, in Ningbo, Zhejiang Province, China, my early life and that of my elder sister and parents was one of hardship. We were desperately poor and constantly struggled to get enough food on the table. This was doubly hard to take considering that, even though we were always short of food, my parents oversaw the operation and maintenance of just over an acre of farmland. In the UK, farming is generally a lucrative industry; in China, it's considered low on the social and economic scale. My paternal grandmother, who lived with us, would often walk down to the river and bring home the dead fish that floated on its surface. When steamed at a high temperature any poison in the fish was killed off, making them safe to eat. But the house smelled of rotting fish while it was cooking. I distinctly recall, in those early years, picking up sugar canes which were discarded in the street, and chewing on the stalks – a risky activity, considering they'd all been in somebody else's mouth. But people make do when they're hungry; they have to.

Nonetheless, a child's imagination, and his freedom to roam, can make up for poverty. We were fortunate to live in an area largely untouched by the industrial expansion which was happening elsewhere in China at the time. The most important time of year for us was the harvest season, during which, as a small child, I was sent to stay with my mother's parents, who lived about eight miles away. Being the youngest in a family of four, I wasn't much help until about the age of seven. I distinctly remember telling myself that I needed to be stronger, that I needed to observe what was happening during the harvest and help my parents.

I remember once, at the age of five, feeling homesick while staying with my mother's parents, and deciding to set off back home, determined to help in any way I could. What I hadn't bargained for were the mountains that lay across my route. These two giants reared up against the sky, covered with wild vegetation, brooks and streams and huge boulders. As the hours passed, I grew tired and scared. Just when I thought I couldn't go any further I was rescued by the army. There was an army camp in the mountains and a worker from the camp found me on his way home.

He looked at me with concern and asked, "What are your parents' names?" My lips trembled and I fought back tears as I told him. A wave of recognition washed over his face – he knew my parents.

"Ah, I know them," he said, sighing with relief. "You shouldn't be wandering around here all alone. There are a lot of wild animals on the mountain and it's dangerous."

He promptly guided me through the labyrinthine paths and took me home. My little legs were weary and my spirit exhausted, the walk home filled me with a strange mix of embarrassment and relief.

For us children, the mountains were our sanctuary. On Sundays, we'd travel up into the wilderness with our backpacks, hauling ourselves up the punishing ascent and carrying with us woks, sweet potatoes and rice cakes. We'd dig for wild vegetables and cook on the woks we had brought from home. In the river, we'd move stones tentatively with our feet, plucking wriggling crabs from their undersides, and catching prawns. We'd build fires and sit around them, chatting, eating and playing. One of my favourite games was hide and seek – our options were limitless, it seemed. We shared this green space with a variety of animals too, some deadlier than others. Alongside the rabbits and birds, there were poisonous snakes, wild boar, pangolin, wolves, foxes, and even – though I never saw one myself – jaguars.

Many years later, I returned to the wild valleys of my childhood and stood in awe of the changes they had undergone. The mountains were destroyed, the rock hacked away to make room for factories and flats. This once untamed, endless playground had been razed to the ground. I stared around me, amazed at the transformation and the logistical power it must have taken, but also saddened at the loss of such natural beauty.

The journey on which I embarked to get here to the UK began in June 2002, but in reality, things were set in motion much earlier. With a good education and a place at university, it was expected that I would enter into a profession, become a doctor or a lawyer perhaps, or take an office job not too far from home, for example, in a management position working for a large Chinese company. I never expected my life to expand and diversify as much as it did. But as soon as I realised there was a possibility for something more, I wanted it. And this, more than anything else, is why I don't believe what the fortune teller said. Although she was right in saying my future was far from home, she could never have predicted the winding path that led me here. It's not about being lucky or born under a good sign; it's about choices and opportunities, seizing them when they come, and creating them when they don't. In the end, my success did hinge on being far from home, but it was also fuelled by hope, a desire for an alternative, and a love of language. Countless hours spent in the library, focused on endless revision and grappling with complex English grammar, proved more decisive than any notion of fate. I could have stayed behind in the village, at the age of 10. Instead, I chose to leave – and the next episode of my life began. I could have spent my adolescence roaming those same mountains I'd loved as a child, completing middle school, then leaving to help my father on the farm. I chose not to and I have no doubt that this was the right decision. I couldn't have spent my adult years there, watching the wildlife and spending Sundays by the brooks. In any case, they no longer exist. That life, once so precious to me, has opened windows onto other vistas. This book is the story of those broadening horizons.

CHAPTER TWO: HISTORY

The history of China in the first half of the 20th century was complicated and brought much deprivation to those living there. I will endeavour to give a brief summary so that you can better understand the events my grandparents and parents lived through and how it affected their lives, and eventually set the scene for my life.

The first Sino-Japanese War happened in 1894 when Japan and China fought for influence over Korea. For China and its Great Qing Dynasty Emperor, the war was a disaster, losing cities and land to Japan. The Qing Emperor of China signed a peace treaty in 1895 ceding control of the island of Formosa (Taiwan) and control of Korea. This defeat ignited political unrest and dissatisfaction with the Emperor's rule and his failure to modernise China. The political opposition was led by Sun Zhongshan (SunYat-sen) and Kang Youwei and this led to the Xinhai Revolution in 1911 and the abdication of the last Emperor of the Qing Dynasty in 1912.

Although a republican government of China was set up in 1912 in Nanjing under Sun Zhongshan, three years later, Yuan Shikai, who was the President of China, declared himself the Emperor of China. The return of an emperor upset many of the regional leaders in China, who also controlled their own military forces. In 1916 with the death of Yuan Shikai, the control of China passed to these various regional leaders (warlords), with no central government.

In 1921, Sun Zhongshan once again established a government in the South of China with the aim of uniting all the regions of China under one administration but he died in 1925. His role then passed to the leader of the army Jiang Jieshi (Chiang Kai-shek), who later married the sister of Sun Zhongshan's wife. Jiang Jieshi took a different approach to the task of uniting China and moved away from Sun Zhongshan's style of inclusiveness and towards hostility to the Communists, which led to the start of China's civil war in 1927.

There followed many years of war, particularly in the South of China between the Nationalist and the Communist forces. In 1931, Japan took advantage of the civil war in China and invaded Manchuria, a region in the northeast of China. By 1934 the Communist forces in Jiangxi province (South China) were surrounded and forced to retreat – this became known as the Long March. Mao Zedong (also known as Chairman Mao) suffered with the people, embarking, with around eighty-six thousand comrades, on the Long March with the aim of breaking through the Nationalist enemy lines at their weakest point. During the march, weapons and resources were carried on men's backs or in horse-drawn carts. The length of this line of troops was around fifty miles, and they usually travelled during the night. During the Long March, they covered a distance of more than resistant to the changing tides; he knew that to obey the rules and follow orders was the best course of action. He was a very intelligent man: in the army, he also worked as the entertainment-group regiment commander and played the harmonica and the flute, as well as traditional Chinese instruments like the Erhu, Dizi and Guqin.

In the 1960s, there were frequent border conflicts between the Soviet Union and China. The Soviet Union border was about 300km (186 miles) from the base to which he had been posted. Their first task was to protect themselves from bombing, which they did by creating shelters using explosives. On one occasion, when my father and other soldiers had to use explosives, the time calculation for detonation was insufficient and the explosion killed two of their own men. My father would often tell me how he was devastated at what happened. He also told me about the extra military training they had to do in case of war. The training included daily target practice and competition to see who could throw a grenade the furthest. Those were hard times. My father told me that the temperature in Inner Mongolia in winter was between −10 and −50 degrees Celsius and he shared an experience where one morning, in those temperatures, the commander was shouting out the orders but the extreme cold seemed to freeze his voice box, much to the amusement of the soldiers. Men's eyebrows and moustaches would often freeze and turn white in the cold. To keep warm, the army huts had stoves and my father told me about one incident in which all the twelve soldiers in one of the huts died from the toxic gas produced from burning coal in the stove. After that, the use of coal was banned and the soldiers had to collect wood from the forest each day.

When Jenny's parents came to collect her, of course, she didn't want to leave my mum as they had developed a strong mother and daughter bond. Both Jenny and my mum cried. My mum accompanied her home to Yinwancun village so that Jenny could be comforted by her on the way home. Many years later, my mum told me that she was terribly sad to see Jenny leave her but, after all, it was in Jenny's best interest to be with her parents.

Although Jenny's parents only lived eight miles away, it was 20 years later, before my mum met her again.

I was born in 1978. I remember my mother telling me that it was in the early morning of the 20th October, which was the year of the Horse, and my mother was dreaming that a Pegasus was flying towards her as I was born. At just 28 days old, I apparently had my first near-death experience. I was sleeping upstairs, covered by a blanket. A neighbour came to visit my mum and when she came back up to check on me – some 30 minutes later – the blanket had almost suffocated me. To her horror, I was unconscious, barely breathing. She undid my clothes quickly and shook me a little until my eyes opened. One of our neighbours went to fetch the village doctor to come to check on me and make sure I was OK and recovered fully. I am extremely thankful that they took the action they did which saved my life.

Things were similarly precarious at our births. While my sister and I were both born in the local hospital, there was no transportation to take my mother there. It would have taken at least seven hours by boat, but three if they walked it. On both occasions, my mother, father and his parents did just that – an arduous, painful journey to deliver us children.

It is very interesting, at this point, to share that in 1979, the year after my birth, the Chinese leader Deng Xiaoping introduced the compulsory one-child policy to control China's speedily growing population which at the time it was about 969 million. If this one-child policy hadn't been introduced, it was forecast that China would have had a population of two billion by 2025.

My mum, aged 18, in 1970

CHAPTER THREE: EARLY DAYS

My earliest memory is one of chaos. I was three or four years old and the river, which ran beside our house, had broken its banks in the two-week monsoon season which is normally from the middle of June to early July. The water raged indoors, bringing with it a collection of fish and – to my horror – snakes. Screaming in terror, my sister dragged me upstairs while my parents and paternal grandmother used long bamboo poles to push the snakes back out of the house. Ordinarily, the river was such a source of pleasure to us, lapping us with its gentle currents, and providing us with fish to eat. Now, it seemed to have turned on us. Some of these snakes were poisonous, and indeed many of my earliest memories revolve around these creatures; cobras that could stand up taller than I could at that age, silent and watching. Once, during the harvest, whilst I was helping out in the rice field, I can remember reacting instinctively, having seen a snake, by taking the sickle I held in one small hand and chopping the snake's head off. If it had bitten me, I was done for. Our village was miles from the nearest hospital, and there was no doubt that without immediate treatment, a snake bite would be fatal. Some poisonous snakes also lived in the trees and if disturbed, they would fall and attack villagers with their deadly venom. A few people from our village died every year from snake bites. But at the end of the monsoon season, normality returned.

Our village, Fangshuicun, had about 150 houses, and a population of about 600 people, most of whom were farmers. Two rivers flowed through the village and it was a 20-minute walk to the mountains. All the roads were made from a mixture of mud and small stones, so when it rained, all the roads became very muddy and slippery. There was a primary school, two small village shops, and we had a visiting doctor. A few friends and I had a favourite haunt, which was on the far side of the river opposite my home. We would go over the river on the stone bridge to this big open safe space, surrounded by many village-built stone storerooms. Some of the open space was used to dry crops and other produce before being sold. This space gave us a lot of room to play. We made our own kites to fly in the wind, plus also making different shapes of paper aeroplanes and doing the same with them. These gave us opportunities to have competitions – how high could the kites get and how far could the paper aeroplanes fly? The storerooms were ideal for games of hide and seek; sometimes it was difficult to find my friends because they had hidden themselves in the hay.

Our home was in a block of six houses, and was a two-storey end terrace, slightly smaller than others. All were mainly made from wood and cement and ours had a total area of about 600 square feet. There were five of us living in this house, me, my sister, my parents and my paternal grandmother. Downstairs had a dirt floor, which was swept clean every morning by our grandmother and I used to practise my marble game there, so I could beat my friends. On this floor, we had a small living room and it was also our dining room. Our mother used this room for her tailoring workshop as well.

The internal walls, made from wood and mud, were papered with newspapers and pictures from old calendars – providing a bit of colour to the rooms. In the spring, swallows would fly in through the open windows to come and nest in the ceiling of our ground floor before laying their eggs. We were always told that they were good birds as they ate a lot of insects which helped protect our crops. The villagers often told us not to hurt the swallows and to look after them. On some occasions, one of the baby swallows would fall out of the nest due to overcrowding. We had to return the fallen chick to its nest. We were also told to take care of frogs as, like the swallows, they ate insects.

We had a kitchen area with a built-in earthenware fire stove (dry straw and wood were used as fuels). My paternal grandmother would go to the mountains every week in order to collect wood. Sometimes I would join her and might come back with a collection of wild fruits, flowers and vegetables. Our home was quite cold in winter, so often the family would gather together to sit beside the stove to keep warm while cooking food. We'd wear thermal underwear and heavy coats inside our house throughout the winter. In order to keep cooked rice dry and last longer, our grandmother used to put it in the bamboo basket with a lid and hang it from the ceiling in the kitchen. If and when we wanted to eat rice, we just got some from the bamboo basket, put it in our bowl, filled it with hot water, then added some soy sauce or pig-fat oil before consuming it. There was also a store room for food, farming tools, and agricultural chemicals.

Upstairs there were two small bedrooms and a balcony. We used to grow chives and small mulberry trees on the balcony. Because we didn't have a bath or a toilet in the house, we had to wash in a basin and relieve ourselves outside or in a chamber pot made from wood which our mum would empty every morning. We did not have a lot of furniture, but there was a square wooden dining table in the living room given by my mother's father and six bamboo chairs made by the local carpenter. In the kitchen area, there was a cabinet and a small wooden table on which food was prepared. We had three beds made from solid wood. (In the summer, we would put a thin bamboo sheet on top of the wooden bed to keep us cool. In the winter, we'd just put a thin layer of cotton blanket on the top of the bed to keep us warm.) Our parents' bedroom had a double bed, a small wooden wardrobe and a table, whilst the other bedroom in which I slept with my sister and grandmother had two beds and one bedside cabinet. As a child, one thing that stood out was that our homes were only secured at night to stop any wild animals from the mountains that might stray inside. The thought of any human being breaking in just didn't figure in our lives.

Beside the back door of the house, the river provided water for drinking, cooking and washing. It was common practice to have a big pot outside for marinating vegetables. With five of us living in the house, we had very little personal space. Our grandmother would do all the housework, cooking and cleaning. My parents would be out working and farming whilst my sister would be in school and I would be at home with my grandmother.

One day, out of curiosity, I went to see our village school, as I wondered how my sister was getting on because I had no idea what she did whilst she was there every day. The teacher was in the front of the class, so I watched both the teacher and students from outside of the classroom window. After this class had finished, I was also curious about the iron bars on the outside of the classroom windows. To see further in, I managed to get my head in between two of these bars, but sadly just couldn't pull it out and was stuck until the teacher found a way to prise apart the two iron bars. He was not happy and word got back to my parents, who were equally upset to be told about the situation, which resulted in me being told off. This still appears unfair to me. How was I, as a five-year-old, supposed to know that if you put your head in between two bars, there was a chance it would get stuck? Once I had experienced this, I was fully aware of the possibility, but at the time it just did not seem like a silly thing to do!

I remember being very unwell, once, when I was six. I had a fever which spiked terribly, and I can recall the intense shivering, the flashes of heat across my cheeks and forehead, the sheets soaked with sweat. The doctor came to my parents' home and told them in no uncertain terms that if the fever climbed any higher, I'd be in serious danger. It is one of the few clear memories, in those early years, that I have of my father. He was terribly worried and, though we didn't have the money, he managed to find a couple of small biscuits for me from one of our neighbours. I remember the heavenly taste as I crunched into them, wondering where he got these sweet treats from. Ningbo is famous as being one of the most important stops on the Silk Road and, as he sat by my bedside, he told me about the silkworms that emerged from warm pouches when coaxed with mulberry leaves. This, I recall, was what drove me to feel better, to become well again. I knew that it was my responsibility to make sure the silkworms living near the mulberry trees beside our house survived. Moments like this only served to confirm for me that we were not well off; that I must be content with biscuits and mulberries forever or seek out something more. Nonetheless, I have never lost that childish wonder. The idea of farming not for the silk, nor the clothes nor the food it would provide, but for the interest of it, the sense of satisfaction, the curiosity it evoked in me. Where does all that silk actually come from, I wondered?

One of the most unforgettable moments of my early days happened when I was seven. Our village was known for its age-old tradition of celebrating the Mid-Autumn Festival, a time when families gather, and children light up lanterns, parading them around the village. The Mid-Autumn Festival, often referred to as the Moon Festival or Mooncake Festival, is a cherished tradition in Chinese culture. This festival venerates the culmination of the autumn harvest, marking a time of gratitude and unity. With the moon at its fullest and brightest, families come together to share mooncakes, express thankfulness for the bounty, and revel in the beauty of the celestial orb that symbolises completeness and prosperity.

While most children had store-bought lanterns, our family's financial constraints meant that I often watched the festivities from the sidelines. However, that year, my grandmother decided to change things. Using old red paper, bamboo sticks, and her knowledge passed down through generations, she taught me how to craft my own lantern. It wasn't just any lantern; it was special. She shared stories of her own childhood as we glued, folded, and shaped. She told me of how she, too, had made her lanterns as a child.

The day of the festival arrived. While other children had perfectly rounded, store-bought lanterns, I had my uniquely shaped, handcrafted lantern. Some children giggled, pointing out that it wasn't as shiny or 'perfect' as theirs. I felt a tinge of embarrassment, but before it could take root, my grandmother whispered, "Your lantern carries our story, our love, and our tradition. It doesn't need to look perfect; it's the heart inside that makes it glow the brightest."

Empowered by her words, I held my lantern high. As the night deepened and we paraded through the village, something magical happened. My lantern's glow seemed to dance and shimmer in a way that the others didn't. It was as if the love and history infused in it gave it a life of its own.

By the end of the night, the same children who had giggled at me earlier approached me, asking if my grandmother could teach them to make such lanterns the following year. It wasn't about the lantern's shape, size, or store-value; it was about the warmth and love it exuded.

That Mid-Autumn Festival didn't just give me a lantern; it lit up a lifelong lesson. True value doesn't come from external perfection but from the love and stories that are woven within.

Learning to cycle was an important part of my upbringing and my first bike, with no brakes, was a slightly battered, second-hand Chinese brand Phoenix and it was very precious to me. I was seven at that time and it meant freedom, independence, the ability to roam, and to explore. I was quite small as a boy, and it was hard to reach the pedals properly. But it was essential I learnt in whatever way I could, as there was no public transportation and the bike granted me the opportunity to travel. Our village was about sixteen miles from the sea, but on our bikes, it was easier to reach the beach and wetland there. My friends and I were a collective, a group of children thrown together by location and circumstance, and we would always come to each other's aid. We were like a litter of puppies, playful and eager, full of energy. For a while, they'd hold on to the back of my bike, pushing me along and encouraging me. When I first got the bike the seat was a little too high for me to sit on properly and one day as my friends pushed me, I lost control of the bike, and having no brakes, I ended up in the river. The bike disappeared beneath me and I feared it would get washed away. I desperately tried to find it, diving under the water. My friends, on seeing my dilemma, rushed to my aid and jumped into the river, seemingly without fear, to rescue and return me, plus my bike, to dry land. My best friend at that time, Chen Jianxiang, made sure I was OK while the others cleaned the mud off the bike. I made them all promise not to tell my parents what happened, in case they stopped me going out on my bike. Regardless of my early tumbles, my confidence grew and I remember the feeling of the wind whipping through my hair, and the exhilaration of realising I had finally mastered my bike.

In the same way, with no lessons, I learnt to swim by clinging to the bank of the river, practising my kicking and feeling my legs grow stronger each day. Eventually, I'd let go of the sides and move out into the open water, joined by friends who either already knew how to swim, or, like me, were still learning. We used to compete to see who could stay the longest under the water and my record was ninety seconds, making me the best.

We never had any money for toys, and I often felt jealous of some of the other boys because they could afford them. However, when I was eight, I grew to be quite an accomplished marbles player, to the surprise to my friends, and I would often swap some of my marbles for other children's transformers toys, which I adored. The car could become a human robot with just a few flicks of its plastic body. I suppose this was an early lesson in strategic thinking and planning, realising that it was possible to transform what you had into what you wanted.

Those early years were an education, though not necessarily an academic one. I could tell you which wild vegetables and mushrooms were poisonous and which were suitable for consumption. I could tell you how we knew a storm was coming, how to build a fire, how to skin a sweet potato and catch a crab. I knew which rivers held the most fish, and exactly what time of day it was best to swim in the cold mountain lakes. I knew how to spot a pangolin and I knew that they loved eating ants and earthworms. I knew when the owls began their nightly hooting, how to cut crops and which times of year the fields would be moist with water. When my sister and I helped our parents on the farm, we'd end the day comparing the number of leeches clinging to our calves, our toes and our lower backs. Everything was competitive, in the friendliest of ways – the leech bites were war wounds and we displayed them with pride. Our childhood was wild and we wouldn't have had it any other way. I remember at the age of eight I would catch eels from the two rivers to sell to my neighbours. Ten eels sold for 50p (5 Yuan RMB). I had been told by my paternal grandmother they were supposedly good for pregnant ladies. I also picked wild herbs and sold them as they were known to be very helpful for anyone suffering from hepatitis. All the proceeds were given to my parents to help with the necessities we needed to live on.

When I was a child, I was very shy. I remember when our family relatives or friends came to visit us, I always ran upstairs to hide because I felt very uncomfortable with my blushing face and sweating hands. My parents used to come upstairs to find me and bring me down to meet the visitors to show my respect towards them. When I was asked a question, I usually didn't know what to say. However, I learnt, as I grew older, not to worry about what other people thought about me and just be myself and I became more confident.

Our family was certainly one of the poorest in our little village of 600 people; most of my friends' parents had more disposable income than us – we had almost none and because of that, some people looked down on us. Nobody was rich, per se, but they were better off than we were. I grew up keenly aware of the different social strata within the village and a clear marker of this was the amount of food each family could afford to buy. My mother would often bemoan the fact that although we grew all kinds of food, we would only keep any items deemed not sellable and all the rest had to be sold. My paternal grandmother cooked for us and there was simply never enough. I always admired people who had enough to eat; ours was a regular diet of rice with soy sauce, sometimes pig-fat oil.

Although my parents both worked extremely hard on the farm, it really didn't bring enough money for the family. In 1980, a new tailoring factory opened in our village and my mother saw an opportunity to escape the low income and high physical labour of farming by switching to bespoke tailoring. This was much more convenient and, crucially, gave us more income and she could still help on the farm after returning from her work in the evening. She would work as a tailor and that meant her leaving the house at 6:00am each day and coming home sometimes as late as 10:00pm. The factory would provide meals for all the tailors every evening. Quite often though, our mum would not eat the meal and bring it back home for us to eat. After three years, when she had learnt to successfully cut patterns, sew garments by hand, put sleeves on suits and dresses, and how to make pockets and stitch the edges of fine garments, she became a Master Tailor. She then was able to make entire bespoke garments by hand – particularly in the period leading up to Chinese New Year, when everyone wore new clothes to symbolise a fresh start. I remember my mum taking me to the factory and sitting me on the floor by her feet, helping her to thread the needles. Sometimes I would end up asleep on her lap as she worked. She was employed there for six years, right up to the time a fire destroyed the factory.

Helping on the farm was important and I would do that after school when I could. My father tended to the land most of the daylight hours and my mother would help him when she came home from work. In the summer, the temperature often reached 38 degrees Celsius. It was so hot in the daytime that they would have to work in the middle of the night until 3:00am. They'd crawl back into bed for a couple of hours then get up and start all over again.

I was lucky that our village was such an agricultural place. We might have been poor, but there was a lot of natural beauty around us. The air was not polluted and in springtime, the world seemed to explode in a mass of flowers and colour. We didn't suffer environmental damage in the same way as many other villages. Heavy machinery and infrastructure seemed to pass us by, for which I'm grateful. It allowed me to be a child for longer.

I think it's hard for most children to appreciate just how much their parents sacrifice for them. For example, when we caught fish in the river and had it for dinner, my mum would always eat the bone and the head. "I prefer it," she'd say, and it's only in hindsight that I can see how much she gave up to give us more. How she hid the discomfort of these privations from our child's eyes. We had very little money to spare, but whatever was left over was spent on my sister and me. While my sister started school at the designated age of seven, I didn't enrol until a year later; we simply didn't have the funds available. I consider, now, how dire their financial situation must have been in the mid-80s and how blessed I was to have had the little money available spent on my schooling. Yes, we were poor, but we could well have been worse

CHAPTER FOUR: FREEDOM

Despite our poverty, it was a happy childhood. My sister and I had our little adventures, picking our way outside in the gloom, and always coming back with stories to tell and delicious things to share. In the evenings, we would go down to the rice fields and ditches, torches clamped in our hands, to catch eels, pond loach and water snails – small offerings for our parents, and a good food source for the coming days. For most people in the village, during the monsoon season, the flooding of the river beside our house was a terrible thing to endure. To me, it was an opportunity for more fishing.

There were times when food was so scarce, we could only afford to buy chicken bones, with a very small amount of meat left on them. Even now, I have a habit of eating chicken bones – they're a good source of protein – even if the idea doesn't sound appetising to most. It's incredible how quickly something like this becomes tantamount to a treat. There were times, too, when we had to rely on the freshly-caught fish, or the wild fruits and vegetables I was able to gather during my excursions on the mountains. Lüshan, Liaoshan, Shuangmanshan and Gaoqian Lindengshan were their names, great, towering giants that seemed like something from another world. On one occasion, my friends and I managed, after two hours, to climb to the top of Lüshan Mountain. From that high point, we could see our whole village and the two rivers which looked quite small from that distance away. When we got back with the wild vegetables, we had collected, I remember rushing to my home to share how we had seen the village from the top of the mountain. My excitement soon evaporated as my parents told me off for going on such a dangerous journey and I never attempted to reach the summit ever again.

The daylight time in our village was a constant, unlike here in the UK, from 7:00am to 6:30pm each day. A typical day for me at this age was getting up at 6:30am, but we had no breakfast as there were jobs to be done. I would go to the mountains with my paternal grandmother to collect wood to burn so that she could cook and pick wild fruits for us to eat. She would tell me which were the good ones that could be eaten and those not to be picked. There was tidying up to be done before my grandmother would prepare lunch, usually at around 11:45am. It was after that I had freedom at 1:00pm each day to go with my friends to play together. I never went anywhere alone at this age and felt having others around me gave me protection and a sense of security. The afternoon always seemed worry-free, knowing there were five or six of us playing together – things like games of hide and seek, looking for eels and just being together were precious times – children being children having fun. Some days would see all of us swimming in the river, or cycling but remaining close to each other and keeping a look out for snakes and anything else that might harm us. I was always thinking of my grandmother's excellent cooking and looked forward to the dinner around 6:00pm when I returned home. Those hours of free play were looked forward to, as my friends and I learnt things for; I guess those afternoons were what I liked most at that age. I never went out alone after it got dark and bedtime for me came around 9:00pm and I would go to sleep full of memories of that day.

I was aware of children older than me going out to the fields and mountain areas to look for snakes. These children would mainly catch cobras and green tree vipers, both exceptionally dangerous because of their life-threatening venoms. The snakes would be brought back to the village after the children had killed them where they would cut them open so they could swallow the gall bladder in one gulp as custom said it contained some medicinal properties for eyes.

The natural habitat around the village was the perfect place to gather food for the family and, looking back, I enjoyed the process. It is one thing to have enough to eat, but quite another to go out and search for it on your own. As the youngest, it always made me feel proud when I was able to do this. It seemed to relieve the terrible pressure my parents were constantly under to feed, clothe and educate us. Children, after all, are expensive.

Our house had a balcony where, most summer evenings, we'd sit together and enjoy the cool breeze. I can distinctly remember seeing lights flashing, on and off, in the distant mountains. "They're the spirits of dead villagers," local people would say, and I shuddered on first hearing this, refusing to go anywhere near them at night. Of course, years later – when we'd moved away, and it had ceased to matter – I found out that the blinking lights were fireflies. After my days capering around the mountains, swimming in their lakes and pools, these were moments of calm reflection, of starry-eyed wonder as my parents told us folk stories while sitting on the balcony. We'd sit, mesmerised, as they described the four great classic novels of Chinese literature – *The Water Margin*, *Romance of the Three Kingdoms*, *The Journey to the West* and *A Dream of Red Mansions*. To describe the contents of these classic novels would need a book of its own to give them full justice. I recall we'd count the stars together and learn about the Big Dipper, Sirius and Vega, and about the fairy stories associated with them, such as the *Cowherd and the Weaver Girl*. This fairy tale is much easier to describe; it is about a love story between Niulang, the cowherd (symbolising the star Altair) and Zhinü, the weaver girl (symbolising the star Vega). The love between them was not permitted by the Emperor of Heaven and, as a result, they were banished to the opposite sides of the heavenly river (symbolising the Milky Way). On the 7th day of the 7th lunar month each year, a flock of magpies formed the shape of a bridge to reunite the lovers for just one day. As a child, these stories were always amusing and very believable.

However, one of my favourite fairy stories was one about a poor young farmer who had not married, but wished he could be. He worked really hard in the fields and whilst doing that he found a large snail in a shell which he decided to take back home with him. He kept the snail in a big water jar. The next night, when he returned home at the end of his work, he found a lovely hot meal waiting for him to eat. He looked around his house, but no one else was there. Whilst eating, he kept wondering who would do such a nice thing for him. The same thing happened for several days and he thought it was the lady who lived next door to him but she told him it wasn't her. So he decided he must find out who was doing this. The next day he left work earlier than normal and sneaked back to the house to peep in to see what would happen. To his surprise, the lid of the water jar opened and out came, not his snail, but a beautiful girl who then cooked a piping hot meal for him before returning into the shell in the water jar. He decided that he needed to know who she was and why she was doing this. So the next day he waited outside the room and while she was preparing the meal he burst into the room so quickly that the girl had no chance to hide. She told him that she was the snail spirit who was here to help him out of compassion for his loneliness and hard work. She asked if she could stay and he answered yes if she didn't mind a farming life of never having much. Not only did she stay, but she also became his wife. Later they had two girls. It is said that they loved each other forever afterwards. This fairy story was my favourite, especially as we were poor, so I went out into the rice field to pick up some large snails and put them in a big water tank at home, to see if the same nice food would be provided for us. That was the power of a fairy tale.

In our village, there was a warehouse-type facility where we had an assigned space for our few family-owned pigs, chickens, ducks and an ox. We had the ox for ploughing and my sister and I enjoyed taking him down to eat fresh grass in the fields and on the mountains. Knowing we were leading him to fresh pastures, he would follow us, trusting in that particular way that animals have. The ox could wander off into the mountains to graze but would normally return by himself. On one occasion, however, that didn't happen and my sister had to go and search for him. After two hours of worrying, she discovered the ox with its tethering lead snagged on the branch of a big tree, which explained why he had not returned. This was a great relief for my sister. We would regularly remove the ticks from the ox's hide after he had been standing in the long grass of the field. Sometimes, the ox would push my sister into the ditch by the side of the field and she'd be covered in mud. I'd help her get out of the ditch and we would both laugh, as it seemed the ox wanted to play with us. Later, we'd head up into the mountains to pick wildflowers for the house, or gather vegetables for dinner. There'd always be a competition to see who could gather the most.

Our days were filled with shared laughter and funny tales. One of my favourites was the 'Great Eel Escapade'. I was about eight and had caught a particularly large eel from the river to sell to our neighbours. Not having a bucket, I decided to carry the eel home in my shirt, gripping it tightly to prevent its escape. However, eels are notoriously slippery, and this one managed to wriggle free, sliding down my shirt and into my shorts. I squealed and danced wildly around our yard, trying to shake off the eel. My sister watched the entire scene unfold, doubled over with laughter. Although it only took a few minutes to finally free myself of the eel, the incident became a staple story at our dinner table, provoking fits of laughter every time it was retold.

We had a small field beside the mountains, about 20 minutes' walk from our home, where, at different times of the year, we grew rice, wheat, barley, watermelons, golden melons, radishes, Zizania Latifolia, Chinese leaf, sweet potatoes, peanuts, tomatoes, sweet beans and aubergines. Autumn was very special. Having watched the crops grow over a period of time, I saw them change from seeds into full grown plants, with a plethora of wild fruits. Mulberries, loquat, and persimmons would ripen, and we'd spend afternoons collecting them. These fruits, with their fresh and tangy taste, became an essential part of our diets. It was desperately hard work for my parents and sister but I can remember delighting in the harvest. The full spectrum of colour was represented there: from deepest purple to brightest yellow, gold and ochre, light pink and dark green.

The Chinese New Year is the most important holiday celebrated in China and by Chinese people all over the world. I remember as a child really looking forward to this time of the year. The celebration was a time for my mum to make new clothes for the four of us, and for me, this was quite exciting. We had to make sure our house was welcoming for our relatives, so my sister showed me how to cut different shapes of animals, using red paper, to decorate our doors and windows. We also had to thoroughly sweep and tidy the house. This was to drive away bad luck and misfortune so we could welcome good luck and good fortune into our home. This we did with all our energy. At this special time, our family would pray to honour deities and give thanks to our ancestors. It was on the Chinese New Year's Eve that all our family would enjoy what was called the 'annual reunion dinner'. The next seven days were for visiting our relatives but more than likely they would visit us, bringing lots of food, as we couldn't afford much. This was good for us as there were always big meals then. For my sister and me, our relatives would give us red envelopes which contained money. Whilst this was exciting for us, we both decided we would pass the money over to our parents to help them. Some of my friends were also very kind to me and would give me some fireworks, which I would let off in the street outside my house. Some neighbours were unhappy because of the noise when they were going off, but other neighbours enjoyed them with us.

During the winter months, the freedom to play outside with my friends was somewhat curtailed. The snow would cover the mountains around us. We did have snowball fights outside of our houses though, which soon seemed to warm us up. The downside to that, for me, was that some of the harder snowballs that hit me left marks on my body the next day. If there was a downfall of snow that was too deep, on a school day, it meant that I didn't need to attend – this seemed very acceptable to me! Most of the second-hand clothes I had, were given to me by my relatives and I was thankful for the thick winter garments. The river would sometimes freeze over and this was great fun for me and my friends. We would ice skate using our shoes, taking care not to go over the thinner parts of the ice. Although on a few occasions we did slip through, this meant rushing home to change, get warm, and receive a telling-off from my parents. It is interesting to note that now the rivers in my village no longer freeze over in winter.

My favourite time of year was the spring season when it felt like nature was waking up. The colours were so varied and beautiful, and the crops in the fields grew tall after months of quiet stillness. It also meant a respite from the rain and a chance for my friends and me to resume our games of hide-and-seek, our mountain-side picnics,

CHAPTER FIVE: OFF TO SCHOOL

I was lucky enough to enjoy eight full years of informal learning before entering formal state schooling. In the UK, children begin the process of academic schooling as young as four or five, but in China, we start at six or seven. I had all those years of time spent with my parents, my sister and my friends, and hours gallivanting through the village, riding my bike, learning to swim. It was a different kind of early education, but an incredibly valuable one.

I started a year later than my peers, as my parents couldn't afford the fees at the time I turned seven. It was tough knowing that my friends were starting their schooling without me, but with all the hope and innocence of a child, I simply waited and hoped. Sure enough, the following year I was able to begin. And what a rude awakening it was. I remember on the first day of the school I went by myself because my parents had already left home to get to work. On the way, I began to feel nervous, wondering what it would be like being in a class of fifty children. I had a number of questions in my mind during my walk – 'how will I get along with them?'; 'will I like the teacher and is he friendly?'; 'how many children from the village would I know?' and 'who will I be sitting next to?' After a short walk, I was at the door of the classroom – this was it, I had arrived. It was nice to be welcomed by the teacher who showed me to a seat at the front of the class, which was the case for all the newcomers. I was really excited to be given a full set of the coursework books and ready to start my formal education.

Our village primary school had just two teachers who had to know about all the different topics we were taught. The age range here was from seven to thirteen as we had to complete six years before we moved on to the Middle School. There were only two teachers who worked in two rooms – Years 1 – 3 in one and Years 4 – 6 in the other. The classrooms had three rows and eight columns of wooden double desks and chairs with two students at each one. These faced a big blackboard and at the back of the classroom, there was another large board to display the best students' work so we could learn from them. With about one hundred children in this school, and only two teachers, it must have been very hard for them to teach that number of students across the three different grade groups!

Most schools in China adopt a rigorous academic schedule. One designed to cultivate discipline, self-control, conformity and – above all – success. We began promptly at 7:00am; we'd recite from the same book for half an hour, our voices rising and falling as one. We'd be expected to memorise certain passages and would be tested to ensure we had learned them flawlessly – rehearsing and practising and trying not to slip up on a word or phrase.

There's a strong belief in China that good health promotes academic achievement so the next item on our daily agenda was morning exercise. As a small boy, I was amazed the first time I encountered it. Just imagine, all years, from 1 to 6, were lined up within their classes to take part in synchronised movements. We'd be given marks on a variety of different exercises, moving from the arms to the legs and the head. It lasted around 25 minutes and we loved it. The whole school was there in the field, about a hundred of us, almost dancing to the loud music blaring from the speakers. After this, there'd be a 15-minute break before the first proper lesson began. Each class lasted 45 minutes – four in the morning and four in the afternoon. At the end of each day, we had to clean the classroom and we'd finish at 6:00pm, exhausted.

Sometimes during class, I would daydream, putting both my elbows on the desk top and supporting my head with both hands under my chin. As the teacher's voice melded into a distant hum, vivid images would fill my mind. I imagined the cool breeze brushing against my face, the scent of pine trees, and the rustling of leaves as I ventured deeper into the mountains. The freedom of scaling heights, hopping from one stone to another over bubbling streams, and the sheer thrill of reaching a peak, feeling like I had conquered my own little world, was so tantalising. The mountains, in my daydreams, became a sanctuary, a place where I could escape the confines of the classroom and the routine of daily life. Every so often, if the teacher saw that I was not concentrating, he would throw chalk at me. It was quite painful and I flinched as it struck my head. He would tell me to stand up for the remainder of the lesson so that I would be more focussed on his teaching. I did, however, find it was difficult to maintain attention during that time as my legs began to ache. At the time, I felt humiliated in front of my classmates, but in the cold light of day, I realised I had been the author of my own downfall.

By the time I started my first year, my sister was already in middle school, so I'd walk to school on my own which took about 20 minutes. It was certainly an intense schedule for such a young child. It only gets worse in high school where students are often working until 9:00pm. Sometimes, during the first years, when I misbehaved, or hadn't recited my memorised passages carefully enough, I'd be held back until 7:00pm. Once I got home, I'd complete around two hours' worth of homework. We'd also have to add to our daily diary, a practice that was compulsory throughout my childhood schooling.

After my walk to school, followed by all that work and exercise, I was ravenous but never had enough money for breakfast. On occasions, my friends might offer me something their parents had packed for them – and sometimes, if I had a little cash, I'd buy something from the street traders. But that wasn't often and my abiding memory is one of hunger; in many ways, I think it fuelled me. In any case, I began to take tiny amounts of sugar from my parents' store cupboard and would pinch it out of my pocket throughout the long day.

At school, I remember one particular game of marbles with a boy who was one year younger than me. I was much better than him and won the game which meant he had to give me the marble he was using. He lived across the river from me and I had a good view of where the had a knock to my confidence. As a result, I was quite undisciplined. Once, during my fourth year, at the age of 12, we were due to have injections. The doctor arrived and I, terrified of needles, went to the front of the class and threw his entire box of medicine on the floor. My mother was called to take me home while the teachers raged about the smashed vaccines.

I found the emphasis placed on rote learning, for example, poems and prose passages, very challenging, and noticed early on that if you could simply recite whatever was written in a book the teachers would praise you. But I just wasn't good at it. Our teachers, frustrated, would beat us with a thick piece of wood when we faltered in our recitals. It wasn't easy to concentrate afterwards, with your hand throbbing and red and unable to hold the pen. When days like this had happened, I was terrified and didn't want to go to school the next day for the fear of it being repeated.

We studied Chinese Literature, Maths, Geography and History. In primary school, we focussed mostly on Chinese history before moving to more international topics in middle and high school. It gave me a good grounding and one I'm grateful for. From a young age, one of my favourite subjects was Natural Sciences. We learned about many different kinds of animals – something that always excited me, given the time I'd spent exploring the mountains and watching fish in the river. I remember staring, open-mouthed, at labelled images of butterflies, incredulous at their intricate bodies and patterned wings. Before I started school, I had, on quite a few occasions, seen 'for real' some of the animals/insects that our teacher told us about and showed pictures of in class. It was great. He would bring some of them into school, non-poisonous snakes for instance, all under safe conditions, and we sometimes would go out into the low mountain areas to carefully catch butterflies using fine nets. Seeing and studying them close up was really fascinating for all of us in his class.

The bond between a child and a pet, especially a dog, is something profoundly special. When I went to school, our dog Guai Guai would follow me and wait for hours outside the building in the blazing heat until it was time to go home. Our neighbour had given him to us as a puppy when I was six years old. We called the little dog 'Guai Guai', meaning 'smart' in Chinese. Guai Guai was a yellow coloured, extremely friendly Labrador dog who grew to be medium-sized. His head was a bit wide, his eyes glimmered with gentleness, and his tail was very thick at the base but gradually tapered toward the tip, like an otter's tail. Guai Guai always wagged his tail happily when he saw me. He used to come to touch my hand gently with his paw to get my attention, making me feel that I was the most important friend in the world to him. One day, when I was nine, he wasn't there when I finished. It transpired he'd eaten some poison, left out for the rats and snakes in the village, and died. I saw my dog motionless outside the school railings. My teacher confirmed he had died and suggested that when I got home I should ask my parents to collect the dog so he could be buried, which they did. It was dreadful, and I can still remember the sadness that surrounded me on the walk home that day. Guai Guai wasn't just a pet; he was a loyal companion, a guardian, and most importantly, a friend. For a young child, this kind of loss can be a first brush with the impermanence of life. Guai Guai's sudden and tragic departure was a brutal lesson in the fragility of life.

As a child, I was utterly captivated by the chickens on our farm. Their life cycle – from laying eggs to those eggs hatching into curious chicks that would eventually mature into chickens – held a certain magic for me. However, this wonder was shadowed by sorrow when it came to the fate of other animals we reared, like the pigs. It pained me every time we had to slaughter them for food or trade. Given my affinity for animals, one might think I'd have aspired to be a vet, yet, in that era in China, such a profession was nearly unheard of. Animals, regardless of their role or relationship with humans, were deemed less significant. So, when a cat met its demise, it was simply accepted without ceremony. Even in larger cities, there weren't any sanctuaries or clinics to turn to if a beloved pet fell ill.

Alongside this early interest, I was also developing a fondness for sports. This was always a welcome break from the more formal studies, and I tried to see how many different sports I could do well. I especially got excited when I represented my school at skipping competitions. The winner was the person who achieved the highest number of skips in five minutes and I was pleased to win a few times. The school arranged for me to come early to train and, as an encouragement, supplied a free breakfast. I was also taught how to play table tennis. We just used two tables from our classroom, a line of bricks for a net, and wooden bats made by one of the teachers – nothing professional at all. I really enjoyed playing table tennis and it later became a very good hobby of mine.

I had survived my six years of primary school education from 1986 to 1992. During that time, I began to learn about some aspects of Chinese history and literature. I was also introduced to information about the Western world, and I learned how to be a good and responsible citizen. School wasn't all bad, but it wasn't brilliant, either.

Me in the front row on the far left, aged nine in 1987

CHAPTER SIX: TURBULENCE

In 1988, my parents decided to separate. This was to have many, many repercussions, but the first and most obvious, to me at least, was the disruption the situation caused to my education. This resulted in me having to attend four different primary schools in the space of six years. Some of my teachers, who knew what was happening at home and were keen to help, were kind to me – even taking me to their homes, after school, to help me improve. I was struggling enormously with my academic work; as soon as I'd settled into one school, I was plucked out of it and forced to begin again.

I wasn't especially close to my father, particularly during this difficult time. To my mind, it was he who was responsible for their divorce, and I felt that, if he had worked harder, the family would have been better supported. We'd have had more opportunities; less fear for the future and more ease in our lives. I felt quite distanced from him as a small boy, and – due to his work schedule and digestive problems – didn't spend nearly as much time with him as I did with my mother and sister.

The days seemed longer back then, with the sun setting on our hopes faster than it did on the horizon. The village buzzed with the chatter of children and the whispers of adults, but at home, an oppressive silence enveloped the air. As my father sat on the old wooden chair, smoking, by the door, staring into the distance, lost in thoughts, the chasm between us grew wider.

Every evening, I would watch as the village children would race to their fathers, jumping into their open arms, sharing stories of their day. I yearned for that kind of connection. A bond that seemed unattainable. My father's presence was like a wisp of smoke – there, but intangible.

His indifference was glaringly evident. It wasn't just his lack of interest in my hobbies; it was that he made no effort to try to understand who I was becoming. But what hurt the most was the realisation that we were like two parallel lines, close yet never truly meeting.

I knew that my parents argued – they tried to keep it from us, but it was almost impossible in our small house. My sister and I heard them quarrelling a lot. That affected us and during those times, to avoid any kind of conflict, I would seek to find an amicable solution. Sometimes, the atmosphere at home upset me, so I would go outside to play. At my age at that time, it was very difficult to fully understand what actually was going on between them. Families need income. They need stability and security. We had nothing on the table and no means to try and change this. Over time, realising that my father's attitude was not likely to change, my mother began to make plans to leave him and move to a town, somewhere we'd be more likely to succeed on a financial level. I know that divorce was the last thing my father wanted. In many ways, I'm sure my mother didn't want it either. But there was no alternative. In her mind the choice was binary: either continue as we were, risking starvation and squandering potential, or move to a better life.

At that time, the law dictated that children chose which parent they followed in the case of a separation. My mother asked my sister and me who we would prefer to follow and we both chose to be with her. She had tried, over and over to make our father change. My mother encouraged him to do more farming, but that seemed to fall on deaf ears. He would sit of an evening smoking cigarettes, an expensive habit that we could not afford, and allow my mother to work the fields, toiling through the night, all so we could have a few grains of rice and soy sauce the next day.

The final straw was when my mother discovered my father had lost the small amount of savings that we had, from selling our farm produce, on gambling. My mother's reaction was to try to drink some poisonous agricultural chemicals that we kept at the storeroom as she felt she could not continue any longer. I was standing there not knowing what to do. I remembered one of the most upsetting sights I had ever seen at around the age of seven – one of the village men with his mouth covered in white froth, from having drunk the same poisonous chemical. He had died on the road. Later, we heard from his parents that he had been depressed, having been turned down by a lady he wanted to be his wife. But she didn't want to marry a farmer, so he took his own life. The realisation that my mother was on the brink of a similar fate was overwhelming. Tears streamed down my face, and I felt a rush of emotions: anger, sorrow, desperation. Fortunately, my grandmother managed to grab the bottle that my mother was going to drink from and pleaded with her. "Think of your children," she implored, her voice trembling. "They need you. You cannot leave them behind." The room was thick with tension, but my grandmother's words seemed to pierce through the fog of despair. Had my grandmother not intervened I am sure my mother would have died at that time, and I am so relieved and thankful that this was not the outcome.

For my mother, moving to a town would provide more opportunities in every way. There were more factories, more work – an economic boom we couldn't have conceived of in our village. My mother was already a qualified tailor by this point and knew she could find a better-paid job in a town to support me and my sister and allow me to continue at school. She could not have remained a farmer all her life. My sister, who had already finished her middle-school education by this point, was offered a job at an automobile repair garage in Qiuai town. She started as an apprentice and was the only female working there.

But life was hard – there is no doubt about it. Divorce was taboo at the time. You seldom even heard the word. I knew, back in 1988, that I'd be looked down upon as a result: by our wider family, my peers and the local community. Nonetheless, the only other option was that I could stay with my father, be hungry, miss my mother and sister, and leave school at the same age as my sister. What would be the use? When my parents were divorced, I, as a 10-year-old, was not one of the causes. But I experienced some of the consequences. Quite often when I tried to join a game during recess or approached a group to make conversation, there was an unmistakable shift. Children would suddenly find an excuse to disband, or their parents would come over, gently but firmly pulling them away. I felt like I was trapped in an invisible bubble, desperately trying to connect with the world outside. As months turned into years, I tried to understand why I was ostracised. Was it fear? Did other parents believe that the "curse" of divorce was contagious, and by merely associating with me, their children would be infected? Or did they believe that since I came from a "broken" home, I lacked morals or was inherently rebellious? The irony was that amidst all these assumptions, no one took the time to get to know the real me. Despite the loneliness and the piercing stares, there was one thing that my parents' divorce taught me – resilience. It taught me to look beyond society's judgments and labels, to find strength in adversity, and to understand that while circumstances may define our path, they don't define our worth.

The constant movement was difficult. I'd already changed from my local village primary to another local primary when the first one closed. Following the separation, I was sent to live with my maternal grandparents for a year while my mother and sister settled into the town of Qiuai. Once they'd been there a sufficient amount of time, I moved once more to a school in that town. This was all within the space of six years and was highly disruptive. It prevented me from really putting down the roots a child needs to thrive.

While I was sad to leave the village, I knew we couldn't continue to live like this. Our house was an extremely basic end terrace cement and wooden structure. It didn't have oil or gas for cooking and heating so we had to use firewood. Snakes and rats seemed to congregate beneath the floorboards and, no matter how many cages we put out to trap them, they always returned. The rats especially nauseated me; they were huge, like small cats, and carried a great deal of disease. When the river flooded, the wood of the house was soaked, and slowly began to rot.

My father remained there after we'd left, and I decided I would not visit him at all whilst I lived at my maternal grandparents' house because I held him responsible for the divorce. All I wanted was to have a life that at least slightly resembled that of my peers: sufficient food to eat, hard-working parents and a father I could admire. I dreaded explaining the situation to my peers – once it became clear that we were leaving. I knew it would bring such shame upon us all. But how could we continue to live in that small, slowly rotting house, as the rats scurried beneath us all night?

I know that when my mother left, seemingly taking his whole life from him, my father regretted his actions terribly. He asked her to reconsider, and promised to change, but we knew her mind was made up. A few years later, my mother remarried, and it was at this point that my father became much more spiritual. He effectively became a monk and was very well-regarded as a master of Feng Shui.

We weren't a religious family. My grandparents on my mother's side were Buddhists and my maternal grandma was the most spiritual. I followed her example as a boy. She only ate vegetables and wouldn't even touch a wok if someone had prepared any meat in it. It seemed that my father's conversion was a result of his sadness.

It seems ironic, now, that he should have such insight into the practice of Feng Shui – the knowledge of the best position for household items; the layout of homes and their general ambience. Such insight is highly sought-after in China, and yet his own home effectively crumbled and led to their separation. He knew that he had to change, but by the time he realised this, it was sadly too late.

Seeing my father's transformation was a bewildering experience. From a man who had, in my eyes, caused the breakdown of our family to one who sought solace and purpose in spirituality, it was a stark contrast. While part of me felt resentment at his earlier decisions, another part was curious about his newfound path.

Every summer, I would hear stories about him, stories that painted a picture of a wise and calm man, who people travelled miles to consult. This was the same man who couldn't hold his family together, but he was now offering guidance on how to build a harmonious environment for others.

One summer, as I was visiting a friend's house in a nearby village, I came across a well-decorated home. The entrance was adorned with red tassels, and the home felt warm and inviting. Inside, the arrangement of the furniture seemed perfect, and there was an aura of peace. I was later told that it was my father's Feng Shui expertise that had shaped the house.

It was then that it hit me – perhaps his expertise in Feng Shui was his way of trying to make amends for his past mistakes. Maybe he wanted to create harmonious environments for others, something he had failed to do for his own family.

I was just 10 years old when my world seemed to turn upside down and I blamed my father entirely for this upheaval. For many years, I was distant from him – upset at the discord and instability he had brought upon our family. I even changed my name from Fan Hongbiao to Wang Biao to adopt my mother's surname. But humans have a wonderful capacity for forgiveness and acceptance. My father had a steep learning curve, and he paid the price for his mistakes. He changed. I changed, too. Whatever happened, he was still my father.

One day, I mustered the courage to visit him. I found him in a modest hut, surrounded by books and scrolls. The air was filled with the scent of incense. We sat in silence for a while, and then he spoke, "I know I failed as a husband and as a father. I can't change the past, but I hope to make amends in the present."

We began to see each other more frequently after that. Our conversations were deep and insightful. I learned more about Feng Shui, and in the process, I also began to understand my father better. He had found a way to channel his regrets into helping others. His spirituality was his anchor in the turbulent seas of his past.

Though the scars of our past remained, our relationship began to heal. It was a slow process, but we both found solace in understanding and forgiveness. The man who had once been the source of so much pain in my life was now teaching me about harmony, balance, and redemption. We steadily developed a good relationship which included speaking on the phone every month, and also sold food, vegetables and fruit. There was also always plenty of work to be found in the fishing industry as sightseers would flock to see the vast expanse of water. My grandparents benefitted from the tourism increase. They saved money by using the lake for washing their clothes and vegetables, and gathering drinking water. They were incredibly careful with their money – and I, a small boy from a broken home, reaped the benefits from those years later. I never had the sense, living there, that our next meal or the possibility of a new pair of shoes hung in the balance.

Yinwancun village school only had one classroom for 45 students, including my Year 3. What a massive difference this was to my previous school of up to 800 students. During my time there, at what was by then my third primary school, I struggled to progress as I spent most of my year there trying to catch up and understand what had been taught.

I started to make friends – but only a few, because my parents were divorced. As I have said, divorce was rare and frowned upon in China, so some parents didn't want their children to be friends with me. Sadly, this was also the case with a few of my relatives. My new best friends were Ma Ke and Chen Jianguo and the three of us used to learn to dance, and play marbles and hide and seek. We'd compete to see who could climb to the top of the hill behind my grandparents' house first – unfortunately, they were too quick, probably because they were a few years older than me. Swimming in the lake beside my grandparents' house became another favourite pastime. We were also successful in catching prawns.

I began to enjoy life again, and looked forward to the

long summer, when the grapes that grew outside my grandparents' house were fat and ripe. Sometimes I'd act too hastily and would cram a handful into my mouth, realising as I did so that they were too sharp. I enjoyed the hours playing each Sunday, but felt that this new place lacked the wilderness of my earlier years. Back at home, I had a sense that the mountains were my own – a stomping ground of which I was king. Here, I was an unknown, a strange newcomer, and the land felt foreign to me – although it was just a few short miles from the house that now belonged solely to my father.

One day in summer, when it hadn't rained for more than two weeks, the dry grass on the hill behind my grandparents' house caught fire. I saw the fire and immediately called my, now, two best friends and we used tree branches to beat the fire out. Later, some adults saw the situation and came to help us as well. The fire was extinguished eventually and the next day the village mayor praised our bravery, which made my new best friends and I feel very proud.

It was a relief to be in a more stable environment after the long months of arguments and the difficulty of my parents' separation. In some ways, too, being apart from my mother and sister allowed me to dissociate from the challenges of life back home. I missed them all terribly and often quietly cried myself to sleep but knew that this was only temporary – one day we'd be together again. My mum and sister would cycle from Qiuai town to Yinwancun village to see me almost once every month when they were not too busy. These visits helped me enormously. It protected me, this separation, from the inevitable sadness my mother would have been experiencing during this time. It would have been a hard thing for a child to see, and in hindsight, I believe that I would have been damaged by witnessing this most difficult period of my mother's life.

My maternal grandparents took great care of me, too, cooking delicious, hearty meals and encouraging me as I began at my new school. I was grateful to be there and loved smelling my grandma's cooking wafting through the window. My grandpa used to warm some milk up and mix an egg in it every morning for me to drink. My grandparents had some savings and, though they caught fish and grew potatoes, they did so in order to sell them, not to survive on them. It felt wonderful to know that there would always be food on the table; that no one needed to worry and that we were safe. It made a welcome change – at home, before, I'd been worried not only about the family's finances and ability to eat, but also for my parents and their marriage. Now, I didn't need to worry about any of these things.

I remember a particular evening, when the twilight glow filled the room, and the scent of jasmine wafted through the open windows. My grandma sat on her favourite bamboo armchair, knitting away, the rhythmic clicking of the needles a familiar background score.

"Do you know," she began, without lifting her eyes from her work, "your mother was a feisty child. But she was just like me." There was a glint of mischief in her eyes. She went on to narrate an incident from her own youth when she'd climbed the village's tallest tree just to prove the naysayers wrong. Her stories were always filled with moments of daring, a subtle lesson on her strength of character and perseverance.

My grandpa, on the other hand, was the quiet anchor of the family. I recalled a time when I was struggling with my studies, feeling utterly defeated. He took me to his workroom, a room brimming with intriguing artefacts and an old globe. Pointing to it, he said, "Life is vast, just like this world. A hiccup here doesn't define the entire journey. Remember, my child, patience and perspective."

Grandma had a habit of reciting poetry as she went about her day. One afternoon, as she taught me to make her famous dumplings, she recited a line that resonated with me, "In the heart's deepest chambers, memories stay; they light our path and show the way." She said it was a line she had penned herself in her younger days, a testament to her depth and wisdom.

Their contrasting personalities were evident in their little banters too. Grandpa's pragmatic approach often met with grandma's poetic vision. Once, during a particularly rainy day, grandpa remarked, "Looks like the crops will flourish this season." To which grandma replied, "And listen to the heavens play their symphony, reminding us of nature's grandeur."

Yet, it was in these contrasts that their bond deepened, each one's strength complementing the other's. The yin and yang, harmoniously existing together.

On some Sundays, I would sing as I cycled the hour each way to visit my mother and sister. I began to see a little more of Qiuai town to which I'd soon be moving. It was good to have this introduction weekend by weekend, rather than all at once. I'd spend the day with both of them before returning to my maternal grandparents' in the evening. It was incredible just how quickly life seemed to have improved for them and I was hopeful for the future. Before the separation, my mother's savings were lost through my father's gambling and she had resorted to borrowing money; we didn't even have enough for watermelon seeds. Now, it certainly seemed like things could be so different, our world was changing and how thankful we were for that. We had moved on.

A scene engraved on my memory in August 1988 illustrates the extent of my mother's selflessness. I was about ten and we were on a summer holiday from school. I'd cycled to see my mother in the tailoring factory. It was over an hour's ride and the sun beat down on my head as I pedalled. My mother was delighted to see me and disappeared not long after I arrived. I had no idea where she was going until she returned with my very first ice cream. I'd never experienced anything like this square, brick-like block of vanilla ice cream. It was everything I wanted at that moment – icy cold and sweet all at once. We barely had the money for one ice cream, let alone two, so my mother smiled as she watched me eat it, but I knew she sacrificed so I could enjoy it. As I write, the memory of my mother's action on that very hot day, when she purchased only one ice cream for me, which was all she could afford, still affects me, to the point of being emotional, and clearly shows how very kind and deeply considerate she was. During my life, I've always tried to replicate those special qualities that my mother possessed which I had witnessed first-hand.

I think, looking back, that I grew up a great deal during this year spent with my maternal grandparents. This was indeed a special time in my life where I grew close to them and I must acknowledge the love, support and care they gave me after what had been a difficult period in my life. Like many children of divorced parents, I matured more quickly than I otherwise might have. I had learnt from my experiences that hard work did not always pay the dividends it was due and that one had to be savvy with one's skills. I was forced to grow from a naïve child to a more understanding, discerning adolescent.

I still remember those care-free days with my maternal grandparents and am buoyed by the memories. Yes, we had endured hardship; yes, I was the child of divorce; and yes, I was struggling at school. But for twelve months none of it seemed to matter as much. I was able to escape what had become the norm and enjoy the last stretch of childhood. Without the separation, I remind myself now, I would not have been able to spend such quality time with my mother's parents: hear their stories, learn their habits and enjoy their company.

It strikes me now that there is so much we don't know – all of us – about the lives of our parents and grandparents. The idea that they existed at all before we came along can seem utterly implausible. My parents' divorce was a tragedy, yes, but it also enabled me to learn more than I otherwise might have. My mother's parents had worked with what nature provided for years. I was scared, the first time, to sit in my maternal grandpa's boat – it was so small, and appeared unlikely to hold our combined weight. They were originally from the city of Shaoxing, about three hours by car from Ningbo, and had escaped by boat during the Japanese invasion. It's no wonder that they regarded the water as a lifeline – it had saved them, time and time again.

Their life had been one of toil and hardship in part due to the civil war and the Japanese invasion. Once they were safely established in the lakeside village of Yinwancun, their lives gradually improved. Chairman Mao had decreed that the mothers of many children (not just one or two) would be hailed as heroines. As a result, my mother was one of seven. Two of her siblings died.

The spirit of acceptance in the face of terrible adversity never left my grandparents – especially my maternal grandpa, who carried on being careful with money into his later life. For example, when he came to visit us in Qiuai town, he would walk the entire four-hour journey rather than spend 5p on the bus fare. I notice the same sense of thrift here in the UK in people who remember the Second World War. There's a frugality inherent in their behaviour, born of years of deprivation and hardship, of never quite knowing when the money would run out, or become worthless overnight.

The lake side where the villagers washed their food, clothes and dishes was incredibly muddy and very slippery and, not infrequently, villagers would slip, fall into the lake and some non-swimmers drowned. This was accepted as an unavoidable part of life in the village until my grandpa decided to take action. He spearheaded a movement to raise £2,100 (21,000 Yuan RMB) to clad the banks in concrete, drastically reducing the number of accidents. He was a very charitable man. People in the village still speak of his generosity and his desire to improve things. My mother learned a great deal from her own parents which she passed down to my sister and me.

The twelve months before I moved to live with my

mother and sister seemed to fly by. My grandma's excellent cooking, kindness and my grandpa's generosity and care have stayed with me through my life. When I look back at the time, I spent with them I feel that all I received from them was just what I needed to help me to enjoy life again, free from worry and family upset.

As the sun set on my time at Yinwancun, I prepared to embark on the next chapter of my life in Qiuai with my mother and sister. The invaluable lessons, tales, and love bestowed upon me by my maternal grandparents not only healed my wounded heart but also equipped me with the fortitude to face the uncertainties ahead. While the village by Dongqian Lake had served as a haven, I was now braced for the new challenges and adventures that awaited. I looked forward with hope, grateful for the sanctuary of my grandparents' embrace.

Me aged 11 on the left, my mum in the middle and my sister on the right, photographed in our maternal grandparents' house in 1989

Me aged 15 on the left, my cousin beside me and my maternal grandparents on the right, outside my grandparents' house, photographed in 1993

CHAPTER EIGHT: OFF TO THE TOWN

When my mum and sister first moved to Qiuai town, they rented a small basic house built from wood and stayed there for ten months before renting a better detached house built from cement and brick. The living conditions and insulation in this house were so much better than any previous house we had lived in. Finally, here was a house free from snakes and big rats. There was a sitting room, kitchen and bathroom on the ground floor but there was only one big bedroom upstairs. It had a long balcony which my mother converted into two tiny bedrooms so that my sister and I could sleep there. This house was eventually purchased by my mother some three years later. She had found a good job as a tailor, in which, even though it was long, hard work she was happy – making bespoke suits, overcoats and dinner jackets whilst making clothes for me and my sister in the process. Her days of farming were over!!

To see our family break up had been too much for my father's mother to come to terms with and one of the worst outcomes of my parents' divorce was that she died heartbroken that the marriage had failed. She had been extremely disappointed and full of sadness both for my parents, and for the impact it would have on my sister and me. I felt so sad at this point because I had lost my dear and kind paternal grandmother. Everyone was very upset and, even as a 10-year-old, I realised that, if I talked to any of my family about the loss of my grandmother, then I would risk upsetting them further. This especially applied to my sister who had been extremely close to our paternal grandmother and I knew the death had hit her hard. So I felt unable to talk to anyone about my feelings at this time which was very hard for the 10-year-old me. I remind myself, now, of how much resilience was required on my sister's part, during the late 1980s. She had left school early; had endured our parents' divorce and the death of a beloved paternal grandparent and had moved to an unknown town with our mother – who was full of her own regret and private sadness. I am eternally grateful for her sacrifice and her tenacity during this time.

After my paternal grandmother passed away, my father moved to Gaoqian town which, ironically, had been the location of my second primary school. I think our old house held too many memories for him. It wasn't until the age of 15 that I saw him next.

By 1989 my mother and sister were ready to welcome me to Qiuai town. It was a wrench to leave my maternal grandparents after such an idyllic year, but I knew that my chances of success and happiness were going to be greater there. I arrived with the same possessions that I had taken to my grandparents' home plus a few extra things they had bought for me to make my new start. I had been to Qiuai town quite a few times visiting my mother and sister. But moving to live with them permanently came as a shock. Gone was a small village and here was a huge town with almost 73,000 people living in just over 24,000 homes. I had to get used to so many differences. There was such a variety of shops: a huge two storey food market, very large supermarkets and a big evening market open between 6:00pm and midnight. The choices had expanded overnight. Buses, with dedicated stopping places, and taxis replaced either walking or cycling. The roads were much wider, made much more solidly and had street lighting. In the morning, the town awakened to a cacophony of bicycle bells, vendors shouting their daily wares, and the distant hum of machinery from the local factories. By evening, the air would cool and carry the comforting scent of home-cooked meals wafting from open windows. All new to me! There was a cinema, a computer game centre, plus a big hospital. I looked forward to using the first two but hopefully never the third!! Another really exciting change from our village was that the town had many restaurants – food was prepared on the premises and people could eat there. Never heard of where I used to live.

Qiuai town was known for clothing manufacturing, tailoring, mechanical hardware and building materials. The town had five different rivers which I used for both swimming and catching fish. Our home had its own indoor water tap and we also had a fridge freezer and washing machine – the age of technology had arrived for us, for which we were extremely thankful. My school here was much larger and there were also other schools in the area as well. Once my mother had saved enough money from her tailoring work, she built an extension to the house which she rented out to a taxi driver and his wife. This worked very well for us; besides bringing extra income, the couple were very nice and would sometimes cook food for me.

On occasions, I would remember the hills and mountains I had left behind, but here there were different opportunities. Our closest neighbour, whom I called 'grandma' because of her age, was so friendly towards us that she would sometimes cook for me. We would eat together when my mother and sister worked late. In many ways, she treated me as her own real grandson. In the summer evenings, I would go and swim with some friends and could be away for more than two hours. This worried her so much that she would come to find me and tell me to return home to study – I wouldn't have it any other way, as she was so caring towards me. How did I find moving from the village to this town? In a word: 'Overwhelming!' But in the most positive of ways. It was here my life was to settle down; my school results improved and our family life finally stabilised. It was as if a huge corner had been turned and my life went from strength to strength.

I attended Qiuai central primary school for Year 4. This was another challenging change as the school had 18 classes, 60 teaching staff and around 1,000 students. Finding my way round such a large school took me some time to get right. Here was the opportunity to improve my learning and grow my knowledge, which began to increase quite significantly. In the spring the school would have a day out, with each class visiting a different place. Twice a year there were sports competitions. The winners of each event would represent our school at a combined school's championship; sadly I didn't manage to win, but I guess being academically strong came first. The time had arrived when study overtook play. I needed a goal, and, because of the difficulty of my early education, my mother agreed to pay for some private lessons in the evening – especially maths – which I was not very good at. My mind would go blank sometimes because I got confused at not being able to follow what was being taught in class. I did find learning maths boring; however, I'm pleased to say, that this situation improved later on in my life.

Within a few months of my arrival, my mother decided that the three of us should go on a Sunday trip to Ningbo city centre and the zoo. This bus journey of about an hour was a new experience for me as I had never been on a bus before. This was to be my first visit to Ningbo city centre and the first time going to a zoo.

Stepping off the bus into Ningbo city centre felt like entering a whole new world. Towering structures, not quite the skyscrapers of modern metropolises, but tall enough to be imposing, stood sentinel to the city's bustling heart. The streets thrummed with a constant flow of people, each moving with a purpose, navigating through the labyrinth of vendors peddling their goods. Stalls burst with vivid colours, from the vibrant reds and yellows of fruits to the intricate patterns of traditional silks.

The air was alive with a medley of scents – the tantalising aroma of street food sizzling on open grills, the fragrant allure of incense wafting from nearby temples, and the unique smell that defines a city: a mix of humanity, commerce, and age-old structures. Sounds melded into a harmonious cacophony: the low hum of countless conversations, the rhythmic clip-clop of rickshaws moving through the streets, the melodies of street musicians playing traditional instruments, and the distant laughter and shouts of children chasing each other.

Every turn seemed to offer a fresh surprise. Historical landmarks, centuries old, stood proudly amidst the urban sprawl, their timeworn facades a silent testament to Ningbo's rich heritage. In tucked away corners, one could find the heart of the city in its teahouses, where the elderly gathered to sip on freshly brewed tea, play a game of mahjong, or simply exchange stories from days gone by.

To me, Ningbo city was a canvas painted with the vibrant strokes of its inhabitants' daily lives, a collage woven with threads of tradition and progress. It was a place where the past and present danced together, and I was there, ready to join in its rhythm.

The zoo was a revelation. Each turn revealed animals I had only seen in pictures. I remember the rush of excitement when I first laid eyes on the giant panda. It sat there, munching on bamboo, its round eyes observing the world with a curious serenity. Its black and white coat was stark against the green backdrop, looking softer than the plushest toy in a store. I felt an urge to reach out and touch it, to feel the texture of its fur, even though I knew I couldn't. There was a profound sense of wonder, but also a twinge of sadness. The confines of the cage seemed too limiting for such a majestic creature. Its vast, soulful eyes seemed to hold stories of lush forests and wide-open spaces, a stark contrast to its current confinement. My heart was torn between the joy of seeing it and the wish that it could roam free in its natural habitat.

It was also nice for me to spend time with my sister. Something that I found endearing about her was that she never seemed to rebel as a child. Even now she always listens to our mother. Psychologically, I think this has much to do with our early upbringing; the fact that mother knew best. Our mum had sacrificed a great deal for us and we would turn to her for advice. I know we're both keen to make her happy above all else and not to disobey her or show disrespect.

One evening, after dinner, my sister and I found ourselves sitting on the balcony, staring at the horizon, lost in our memories. The dim light from the streetlamps below filtered through, casting a soft glow on her face.

"You know," she began hesitantly, her voice quivering slightly, "I still dream of our grandmother sometimes. I see her in that old kitchen of ours, preparing that special soup she used to make for us."

I nodded, memories flooding back. "With those big chunks of chicken bones and the herbs she'd pick fresh from the mountain," I added, grinning.

She chuckled, "Yes, and she'd always tell us about how those herbs would make us strong and wise. I never really understood what she meant by wise."

I thought for a moment before replying, "I think she meant that with good food and love, we'd grow up to make the right choices. To be kind, to be understanding, to cherish the memories and learn from the past."

Tears formed in her eyes. "I miss her so much. She was always there, you know? Even when things got tough with our mother and father, she was our constant."

I reached out, taking her hand in mine. "I miss her too. But every time I think of her, I'm reminded of the strength she had, the strength she passed onto us. And it gives me hope."

She squeezed my hand, "She'd be so proud of us, you know?"

I nodded, "I know she would be. And in a way, I feel like she's still with us, guiding us, watching over us."

We sat there for a while, lost in our thoughts, comforted by the shared memories of our beloved grandmother.

Nonetheless, I entered my early adolescence with a slightly more rebellious streak. I'd lose track of time easily and would often realise to my horror that it was gone 9:00pm and I had been out with my new friends playing hide and seek for hours. Despite my plans to expand my knowledge base and work even harder at school, I was a naturally playful boy and was reminded, on more than one occasion, that my mother and sister were sacrificing a great deal to put me through school. My mum had only completed one year of primary education and was desperate that my schooling would prove more comprehensive and open up a variety of doors for me. It must have been hard on them both when I scuttled home at night with my clothes dirty from the day spent with friends. On one level they wanted me to integrate with our new community, to make pals and enjoy my time off with them, but on another, any moment playing was a moment away from my textbooks. I had already fallen behind as a result of the moves and the instability.

As the days turned into weeks and the weeks into months, Qiuai town began to feel like home. I had started to carve out a new life amidst its bustling streets, and the memories of my village, while never fading, started to become threads in a tapestry of new experiences. But as settled as things seemed, the winds of change were once again stirring on the horizon. Unbeknownst to me, life had another twist in store, one that would challenge my newfound stability and reshape my future in ways I could never have imagined.

CHAPTER NINE: THE WEST

The Chinese system of education is comprehensive and wide ranging but rigid. Its main aim is to expand the knowledge base of its pupils in order to fuel the country's economy. Much of our learning involved spoken repetition – hours and hours of it – and endless rote copying. We were expected, at all times, to hold China and Chinese values at the forefront of our minds. There was not much room for deviation from the norm, for spontaneity or for learning about a topic in a novel or exciting way. Science and technology are highly valued as any nation which is able to excel within these fields will inevitably attract foreign interest, buyers and national income.

The British school system can be similarly rigid with its state school national curriculum. But there seems to be a great deal more allowance made for the individual – I was struck by the wide variety of subjects available for students to study here in the UK, including such non-mainstream topics as Horology, Ethical Hacking, Baking Technology Management, Animal Behaviour and Psychology, Surf Science and Technology, and Contemporary Circus with Physical Theatre.

Coming from a poor background, with so few connections, I knew that the only way to succeed was through education. Nonetheless, I knew from an early age that I did not want to specialise in a technology-related subject or dedicate myself to mathematics. I wanted to become a successful businessperson in order to help my family financially. To achieve this, I knew that proficiency in the English language would be a great advantage. For me, making a success of my life was as much about seeing the world, expanding my horizons, as it was about the career itself. A businessperson based in China would make a good salary, would be able to provide, would ensure a degree of stability for themselves and their family that would last a lifetime. But an international businessperson could achieve all this while seeing the world. I knew from what I had seen on the TV, read in the news and from books, that there was a bigger life outside my village, my province, my country – and that I had yet to see any of it.

In 1992, at the age of 14, I started middle school, and what was to be a defining time in my life. Dongyudi middle school had 17 classrooms, each with around 65 students, and a teaching staff of 57. The school was in the centre of Qiuai town, and it took me about 20 minutes to walk there. It didn't take long for chemistry to become my 'least liked lesson', but I thoroughly enjoyed English and Chinese literature. This was also helped by learning songs both in Chinese and English.

Ms. Liu, the English teacher I had, went beyond teaching us the four core English learning skills of listening, speaking, reading and writing, which it was important to fully understand and master. Ms. Liu incorporated learning about the Western culture which provided a context that helped me grasp some of the intricacies that were at first hard to understand. This, however, made me realise that I wanted not just to learn the basics of a new language but to improve sufficiently in all aspects of it to support my future hopes of exploring the West. (On reflection, I found the teaching of Western culture that I received was rather old fashioned compared to that which I experienced on my arrival in the UK.) She taught the cultural differences between China and the West, which improved our English thinking ability and cultivated our cross-cultural awareness. Had I been born, say, 15 years earlier this method of teaching wouldn't have been in place, so I count myself very fortunate as my route in life could have been so very different without it.

Ms. Liu was not just any English teacher; she had a unique way of making the English language and Western concepts come alive for us. I still remember a lesson when she brought in a collection of Western fairy tales. To explain the concept of irony, she read out "The Emperor's New Clothes." She then facilitated a discussion about how societal pressures can often blind us to obvious truths, drawing parallels to our own culture.

But what truly set Ms. Liu apart was her patience with students who struggled. I recall a classmate, Jun, who had difficulty grasping idiomatic expressions, such as "it's raining cats and dogs". Instead of dismissing him, Ms. Liu held special sessions after class where she used local tales and folklore to explain these complex English phrases. By connecting English idioms to stories we were familiar with, she made the language more accessible.

Moreover, when students found it hard to relate to certain

Western concepts, she would bridge the gap by drawing comparisons with our own traditions and values. Once, when teaching about Western individualism versus collective societies, she compared it to the Chinese principle of 'jia ting', or family. This made the concept instantly relatable, helping us see that despite the differences, there were underlying similarities in human values across cultures.

In Ms. Liu's classroom, language and culture were not just subjects to be studied, but windows into a world beyond our own. Through her innovative teaching methods and genuine care for her students, she instilled in us not just knowledge, but curiosity and empathy.

Since I was both enjoying and progressing so well with learning English, my mother decided to pay for private English lessons after school. I also began to learn even more about the West and Western culture by reading newspapers and listening to the BBC World Service. We were fortunate by this time to have a television at home. It was because of my real interest and enjoyment of English lessons that my position in the class improved greatly which certainly pleased my mother and sister.

I became really good friends with three fellow pupils from the school, Chen Zheng, Jiang Hui, and Wang Qin. Outside of school time, we enjoyed testing each other with our newly learnt English words. When we were using English words, bystanders would have a puzzled look on their faces because they could not understand what we were saying. It felt almost as if we had invented a new secret language. We felt a sense of pride that we had the confidence to practice and use English words other than those we had learnt in our classroom.

We used to have picnics with sweet potatoes and rice cakes. We would play near the railway and sometimes destroy wasp nests under the rails even though there was always a good chance of getting stung for our troubles. In hindsight, this was clearly very dangerous and not to be recommended today to anyone. However, in those days we were young and unwise, although if we heard a train coming we would quickly move off the rails. We'd swap electronic games, play cards together, go to the cinema and swim in the river. It felt wonderfully liberating to be gone from my home village where everybody knew my family and where we had been so poor. Now, we had a little extra money which enabled us to enjoy life, rather than simply to exist. I no longer had to rely on stolen pocketfuls of sugar or the generosity of my friends. It was a school rule not to visit the local computer game centre, but one evening I did get into trouble when one of the teachers caught me playing on one of the electronic games when I should have been at home studying and doing my homework. The following morning, as a punishment, I was told to stand in our teacher's office for an hour and had to promise not to return to the computer game centre again. I can honestly say I did feel very ashamed because I felt I let myself down and I have not had much interest in 'computer games' since that time.

When I was 16, the routine of Qiuai town's daily life was interrupted by the presence of three Filipino engineers: Alfredo, Joe, and Marlon. Their unfamiliar faces stood out at a market stall as they grappled with the linguistic barriers, trying to explain their needs to a bemused stall owner. Sensing their frustration, I approached, realising this was a golden chance to practice my English.

"Need some help translating?" I offered. The relief was evident in their eyes as they gratefully accepted. With my assistance, they not only purchased the coat they were eyeing but also got a glimpse of Qiuai's charm when I volunteered to be their tour guide.

It wasn't long before our initial interaction evolved into a deep-rooted friendship. Alfredo, with his jovial anecdotes, Joe's insights into Filipino history, and Marlon's tales of their home islands, introduced me to a culture that was both distinct and fascinating. Our weekends were characterised by a mix of English lessons, shared meals, and cultural exchanges. I would listen with rapt attention to their stories, each narrative painting a vivid picture of life beyond Qiuai. Their accounts offered a richness and depth to my understanding of the world that textbooks couldn't capture.

Moreover, their presence and our subsequent bond became a significant catalyst in my English learning journey. Our conversations were the perfect practical lessons. I not only improved my linguistic skills but also began to understand the nuances and cultural undertones of the language.

Qiuai's residents were initially wary of these outsiders. However, through our interactions, many townspeople began to see the engineers not as distant foreigners but as friends who brought a slice of the world to our doorstep. In doing so, they indirectly nudged me to reflect upon my own culture and traditions, viewing them through a new lens, one that juxtaposed them with the broader world.

Our bond endured the test of time and distance.

Today, our conversations continue on digital platforms, a testament to the enduring nature of friendships that transcend borders. The time spent with them did more than just improve my English; it reshaped my aspirations, reinforcing a fervent desire to explore the world and immerse myself in diverse cultures, starting with my dream to study abroad despite the lack of resources and connections.

It was not expected that I, a child from a small and poor agricultural village, who had begun his education a year later than normal, would do anything as aspirational as learning English to a professional level so he could go abroad. I hasten to add that it's not as though this was seen as an unworthy ambition – just inconceivable to anyone I could have shared it with. To go overseas and become a success using the English language I had learnt at school was an achievable plan but emigrating required money that we did not have. To devise such a plan within my financial constraints seemed implausible. I stayed focussed on my dreams and ambitions by holding on to the hope that where there was a will then there would be a way.

The older I become the more this fundamental fact is confirmed; with money in the bank, life is rendered easier. Not easy – it's never that simple – but easier. For so many people a lack of wise investment leaves them unable to realise plans, hopes and dreams. Here in the UK, the prospect of purchasing a home over the years has become harder, even for those on good salaries with a decent education. Western economics divides those who have from those who have not. Let's take the lives of two children, one born in an affluent area of north London, the other in an impoverished suburb of a northern town. One may attend a small private school, with fewer students per teacher than in the state-funded education system. That one may learn ancient languages, take exams early, be involved in a range of extracurricular sports, music lessons, travel the world and – by the time they're ready to apply to university – have interview coaching and lots of experience of interest for their application forms. The other child may have to rely on free school meals, have access to none of the same extracurricular activities, all of which cost money, and may not even leave the town in which they were born. Their horizons, as a result, grow smaller each day while those of the London child will expand.

While I may not have fully understood this as a child, there were fundamental obstacles to me achieving my goals. I knew that Western capitalism served those who worked hard and who were predisposed towards success. What's more, affluent children – here in the UK or in China – are exposed more readily to the sorts of opportunities and life choices that invite success. "You can't be what you can't see", as the old saying goes, and what I could see was a struggling family, parents who worked around the clock for little financial reward, and hardship. It didn't seem possible, even if I were to become proficient at English, that it could take me anywhere beyond the village and the life I knew so well.

There was added pressure too, and I felt the weight of the responsibility, particularly because my sister had chosen not to continue her education past middle school. She made this sacrifice, allowing me to pursue my academic aspirations. Fully conscious of her selflessness, my ambition to excel in English and overcome my challenges intensified. Her sacrifice underscored the gravity of my pursuit–not just for my own sake but for our family's future. With such high stakes, the pressure was at times overwhelming, like navigating through a thick fog. Yet, this same pressure honed my determination, reminding me daily of the promise I needed to fulfil.

I had barely any concept of life outside the village during my very early years. The move to Qiuai town had widened my horizons and we were encouraged to enquire into more than we were taught in school. I can remember being fascinated by any story, or news item on the television and radio, that featured the West, and especially the UK and USA. That small island adrift from the mass of Europe seemed to be constantly making headlines. I knew there was a great deal of economic opportunity there and that it was a land of gentlemen and ladies, of polite "pleases" and "thank yous". I understood it to be a place of high standards and a high quality of living. Slowly, very slowly, an idea began to filter through my mind that a degree from an overseas university might improve my chances of gaining a good job in China.

My dream, as a child, was to succeed in a good job and eventually to become a businessman. I had no idea how to achieve this as I was without connections, without links and introductions or any real knowledge of how the business world turned. But I did know that hard study and perseverance were the first steps. Even then, despite these ambitions, I never expected to run my own business; this would have seemed too great a leap.

As an interesting footnote to this chapter, I recall the

rebelliousness of some of my peers. Those in gangs liked to stage fights before and after school. I tried my best to follow the rules as I was keenly aware of the importance of completing my exams and moving on. One of the courses we began at this time called "Ideology and Morals" was a particularly valuable one. It essentially taught us to respect public property, to contribute to the greater good, to help our neighbours and not to damage public facilities. When I see the smashed windows of telephone boxes, or the graffiti on street walls in the UK, it strikes me such an education might be valuable here considering the respect Chinese people have for communal areas. The Chinese system of education may seem odd to a Westerner, but there is a lot of good to be found within it.

Reflecting on this transformative chapter of my life, it's evident that my education was more than just rote learning or passing exams. It was a window to the vast expanse of the world, a kaleidoscope of cultures, thoughts, and experiences that existed beyond Qiuai town's borders. My interaction with the English language and the cultural vignettes it brought with it, especially those encapsulated in my time with Alfredo, Joe, and Marlon, gave me a glimpse of "The West"–a realm that felt both tantalisingly exotic and surprisingly familiar.

My education, in many ways, reinforced my growing aspirations. The stories, the languages, and the interactions with people from lands I'd only read about made me yearn for more. They instilled in me a thirst to not only learn about the world but to actively engage with it, to be a part of the global narrative. I wanted to be someone who didn't just consume stories but contributed to them, adding my unique perspective as a product of my upbringing in Qiuai town.

Now, with the vantage point of time and distance, I look back at those days with a mix of nostalgia and gratitude. They were my formative years, a period where dreams took root, aspirations soared, and a young mind realised that boundaries were merely lines on a map. My world, once confined to the perimeters of Qiuai, had expanded infinitely.

The 'West' for me was not just a direction or a geographical entity; it represented possibilities, a horizon that kept extending the more I pursued it. And in that pursuit, I didn't just discover different cultures or languages; I discovered parts of myself that I hadn't known existed. It's a journey that began in the heart of Qiuai town and, in many ways, continues to this day, as I navigate the ever-evolving landscape of my dreams and aspirations.

CHAPTER TEN: DECISIONS

In 1995, I started high school and chose to go to a leading military-style boarding school which had a good reputation for academic achievements. Those final few months of middle school proved to be the last time I'd ever live with my mother and sister. They had put their savings together to pay for this next, most privileged step for me. Wuxiang High School, a co-educational boarding school, had 16 classes with about 900 students and 75 staff.

The initial two weeks at Wuxiang High School were perhaps the most intense and challenging of my entire educational journey. Before diving into our academic pursuits, we were thrust into a rigorous military training programme, designed not only to instil discipline but also to build a strong and healthy body.

Every dawn, as the first rays of sunlight pierced the horizon, we were roused from our slumber by the sharp blast of a whistle. The morning routine was non-negotiable: a series of callisthenics, jogging sessions and formation drills. We donned our military green uniforms, the fabric stiff and slightly uncomfortable, but the feeling of unity it fostered was undeniable.

We were taught basic marching techniques, the importance of obeying commands without hesitation, and how to work as a cohesive unit. Our instructors, stern-faced and unwavering, were strict but fair. Their main aim was to break down individual barriers and build us back up as a single, unyielding entity.

But more than the physical training and learning discipline, it was the internal transformation that stood out. We learned the value of persistence, resilience, and the importance of placing the collective above oneself. This training was not just about moulding soldiers; it was about crafting responsible, disciplined citizens who would carry these values into their futures –whether in academia, professions, or personal endeavours.

The military training, while short-lived, left an indelible mark on us. While it was a departure from traditional classroom learning, the life skills it imparted were invaluable. It served as a potent reminder that before we could master our academic pursuits, we first had to master ourselves. And as the years at Wuxiang High School unfolded, the lessons from those first two weeks became the bedrock upon which I built my high school experience.

The teaching staff also lived in the school. My dormitory was about fifteen feet long and twelve feet wide with five sets of bunk beds for the ten of us who shared the room. I was allocated one of the top beds. Our breakfast, lunch and dinner were served in the canteen where we had to stand to eat as there were no chairs. We did have one shop we could purchase some things from.

We had to abide by all the school rules: arriving in the classrooms five minutes before the class started; no running within the building; no shouting; wear the uniform all the time; no boyfriend/girlfriend relationships (some, however, did have secret relationships, including myself); sweep the classroom at the end of the lesson; and make sure that our dormitories were kept clean and tidy at all times. We were only allowed to go home once every month unless we were ill. There needed to be written approval from the head teacher in order to leave the school to go home or to see a doctor; otherwise students were not allowed to go outside. Boys' hair had to be kept at less than 6cm and natural. Girls' hair had to be natural, with both high heel shoes and makeup being banned. No one was allowed to play computer games, go to bars, drink alcohol, smoke, or swear. We had to adhere to the rules and work hard. The enforced strictness made it different from my previous schools and good behaviour was rewarded with points so it was important to do your very best. After all, we were all aware of the strict rules before we started there.

My mother and sister were determined that I succeed, and progress to university, gain a degree and enter a well-paid profession. The school was an hour's cycle ride from Qiuai, which was no great hardship, but we were not allowed to leave – even at weekends. We had lessons from 6:30am until dinnertime, after which there was private study. We were sent to bed at 9:00pm. That was seven days a week! The school had a reputation for its rigour which was justified by gaining places for many students at some of the country's most prestigious universities. Like everything else, though, this came at a price.

I cannot say I enjoyed my time there, but I certainly benefitted from it. I found my teachers too strict and I felt isolated. I missed my family. Early in the morning monitors came to inspect the folding of our blankets, check the positions of our pillows and calculate points based on every student's presentation. It was a system of strict quality-control, and it's incredible to reflect on how quickly this became the norm.

Thankfully, I made friends – Cui Hongliang and Xia Ning, for example – and together we'd sometimes climb the school wall, head off to the cinema or buy something to eat in the evenings.

One evening, whispers spread through the corridors: 'Titanic' was screening in a nearby cinema. To students like us, who had limited exposure to Western films, the opportunity was tantalising. Xia Ning, who loved a bit of mischief, was the first to suggest we venture out. Cui Hongliang was initially hesitant, but the allure of the experience was hard to deny.

We chose a Saturday evening for our escapade, thinking our absence might go unnoticed amidst the weekend chaos. We traded our uniforms for casual clothes, giving us a slightly better chance of blending in with the city crowds.

With the cloak of night as our cover, we scaled the school walls. The world beyond was exhilarating, a blend of fear, freedom, and adventure. At the cinema, we were transported into the heart-wrenching story of Jack and Rose, feeling their love and loss deeply.

But the real hard part came after the film was over. It

was very important to get back into the school without anyone noticing. As we approached the walls, a guard's flashlight pierced the darkness near us. We ducked and hid –our hearts pounding so loudly we were sure it would give us away. Thankfully, he moved on, and with bated breath, we made our way back inside.

While we never spoke of our secret cinema outing, that night represented more than just a film. It was a fleeting taste of the freedom and world beyond the school walls we so yearned to be a part of. It felt good to be normal children, just for a little while. Whilst I've said I didn't enjoy my time there I have to acknowledge that it did teach me to be self-disciplined and independent.

Academically, we were expected to work as hard as humanly possible and excel at every one of our courses: from Chinese Literature to Maths, English, Physics, Chemistry, History, Geography, Biology, Ideology and Morals, Art, Music and PE. My favourite subject remained as firm as ever – English. We were also set daily eye exercises to prevent our sight deteriorating after all those hours of study. Nonetheless, when I was disciplined (and I was disciplined often), it was usually because I had stayed up after lights out to read and try to improve my marks. I'd pore over the pages of my textbook with my torch burning bright to ensure I scored well on the following day's exam.

We were graded on our behaviour, too; I once had a point deducted for running in the canteen when I was too hungry to wait for lunch. Our uniforms were expected to be pristine. They were blue and red and the very thin jacket provided little relief from the cold in winter. I don't remember excelling at anything in particular. I was either

Position in the family hierarchy is very important in China. Confucius taught that showing respect to one's elders was the most important thing in relationships. The elderly not only included parents but also grandparents, aunts, uncles, and teachers – basically any relatives or friends that are older than yourself. To show respect to the elderly, one should obey them in all things and accept everything they say as correct.

In Chinese culture, people believe that showing affection can pull people closer without any consideration for age, experience or background. By saying, "I love you" to their children, parents may feel they are getting too close to them which could suggest they were equals – completely against the traditional culture of parents maintaining their power which comes from their place in the hierarchy. Chinese parents feel they should not be "friends" with their children, as they need to be parents 24/7 so should not put themselves in a position of losing face. My mum doesn't really follow this tradition very well as she is always hugging people.

My mother told Jenny about all the ups and downs of her life which had led to the move from Fangshuicun village to Qiuai town. Jenny was sad to learn about the divorce but, at the same time, she was delighted to hear that my mum had remarried. Jenny didn't know I existed at all because I was born ten months after she went back home to her parents. My mum wanted to know everything that had happened to Jenny since she was a baby and was very proud that Jenny was working for a foreign company which was much better paid than working for a Chinese company at that time. My mum was also very impressed that Jenny had a company car with her own designated driver.

They kept talking till midnight but my mum knew Jenny had to go to work early the next morning so she let Jenny go home. Jenny said that now she knew where we lived, she would come and visit often. They hugged each other again before Jenny and her mother left.

Jenny would come over to our house in Qiuai town almost every month and established a close relationship with my mum and my sister Tiejun. I was in boarding school so never got to meet Jenny. Later that year mother moved to Hangzhou, but Jenny would often meet up with my sister and sometimes stayed over. For Jenny, Tiejun became the sister she had lost when she was very young.

It was as a result of my stepfather's connection to Hangzhou that I was introduced to the city and applied to the university there. Hangzhou is the capital of Zhejiang Province and in the 12th century was the capital of China. Marco Polo visited Hangzhou in the late-13th century and in his book he records it as "The City of Heaven, the most beautiful and magnificent in the world." Following my mother's remarriage and her move to the city, I could see much more of her when I wasn't studying. Though I lived in a college dormitory, she and my stepfather weren't too far away.

I moved to Hangzhou two months prior to the start of my university course. My stepfather gifted me a PC, complete with speakers, a scanner and a printer. It cost around £1,200 (12,000 Yuan RMB), which was at least three months' salary for him.

A colleague of my mother who was a computer technician very kindly accompanied both myself and stepfather to make the purchase. I learned quite a lot from him because we had to assemble the computer once we got back home. The first time I laid eyes on the assortment of parts that would eventually form my PC, I felt a mix of exhilaration and apprehension. It was like staring at the pieces of a jigsaw puzzle, each component waiting to find its rightful place. In an era when many of my peers had never even turned on a computer, having one felt like holding a piece of the future right in my hands.

Assembling it was both challenging and revelatory. Every chip, wire, and screw had a specific role, and ensuring each part connected correctly was a lesson in patience and precision. With the guidance of my mother's colleague, I began to understand the heart and soul of this machine. Each successful connection was like a mini triumph and, with every step, my respect for the intricacies of technology grew. By the time we powered it on and heard the familiar hum of the PC, I was awash with pride and a newfound appreciation for the marvels of modern engineering.

The idea to develop a tourism website about Hangzhou came naturally. The city, with its rich history and breathtaking landscapes, had captivated me since my arrival. I wanted to share its beauty and allure with the world –especially those who might not have an opportunity to experience it firsthand. I envisioned a platform where tourists could learn about the city's landmarks, its vibrant culture, and even its lesser-known gems.

Creating the website was no small feat. Web development was still in its infancy, and resources were limited. I poured over books, learning about HTML coding, graphic design, and how to optimise the user experience. Challenges arose at every corner, from deciding on the website's layout to ensuring it was user-friendly for people of all tech proficiencies. But every hurdle was a lesson, teaching me resilience, innovation, and the art of problem-solving.

One particular accomplishment was integrating a virtual tour of the famous West Lake. Through a combination of photos and descriptive texts, I tried to transport visitors to the serene waters and lush surroundings of the lake, allowing them to experience its beauty from thousands of miles away.

The website became more than just a project; it was a manifestation of my love for Hangzhou and my passion for technology. It symbolised the bridge between the traditional and the modern, and through it, I felt I was contributing a chapter to Hangzhou's evolving story.

The knowledge gained from this exercise was to prove very useful in the future when I worked at an Internet Cafe. Once Windows 98 was installed and I had attended some training my computer skills improved rapidly. I was able to make good use of the internet to keep up with foreign news, especially in English. My stepbrother was in the army and my stepsister was married so, at the weekends, I would return to my stepfather's, where the PC was kept, to make full use of it, even though it was about one and a half hours away by bus.

My first weeks as a university student were a challenge. I had come from a small country village, to a lakeside village, to a larger town, and now a major city; it certainly took some adjustment. At my middle school there'd been no more than 1,100 students and, at high school, 900 at most. At university, the facilities seemed endless, and the site was sprawling – almost like a small town itself. My childhood days had been full of mountains, water and exotic animals. My university days started full of apartments, towering skyscrapers, and more shops that I would ever have time to visit. I was one of the 20,000 students at Hangzhou Normal University – a figure that gives some indication of China's size. Its population is 20 times greater than that of the UK. I was keen to make friends from the start, but I didn't know a single soul. I forced myself to overcome my shyness by joining the English Club where all the conversations were in English. I was determined to master English grammar.

I remember sitting on the train on that first day knowing I was speeding towards a better future. Those first days passed in a blur: a kaleidoscope of new faces; shopping for necessary items; speaking to new people; and generally adjusting to life outside the regime of Wuxiang High School.

University, for so many people, is a time of excitement and self-discovery. I was no different and threw myself into this new way of working. Whilst I was learning my mind was full of the endless possibilities opening up to me. Each day I was improving and gaining more knowledge.

The world of literature opened up new horizons for me, offering glimpses into cultures and times far removed from my own. It wasn't just about the stories but the very fabric of these tales, the underlying ethos, the character struggles, and the societal commentaries that resonated deeply.

Charles Dickens, in particular, became a guiding star in my literary journey. One of the passages that forever imprinted on my mind was from "A Tale of Two Cities": "It was the best of times, it was the worst of times..." These lines encapsulated the dichotomy of life, the juxtaposition of hope and despair, and it made me reflect on the contrasting worlds I had witnessed, from my humble village beginnings to the bustling urban life of Hangzhou. Dickens' portrayal of the grit and spirit of the lower classes, as seen in characters like Oliver Twist, gave me a sense of the universal struggles for basic dignity and rights. I was so moved by 'A Christmas Carol' and the idea of bestowing charity on those less fortunate than oneself. It was a revelation of the shared human experience across cultures and time.

Jane Austen's works offered a different kind of enlightenment. The intricate dance of manners and societal expectations in "Pride and Prejudice" was both alien and fascinating. Elizabeth Bennet's assertion, "I am no bird; and no net ensnares me; I am a free human being with an independent will," became a rallying cry for my own aspirations. It underscored the value of individuality and self-determination, values I held dear as I charted my own course in life. Austen's keen observations on relationships, class, and societal norms made me curious about the nuances of English culture, its subtleties, and its stark differences from my own upbringing.

Both Dickens and Austen painted vivid tapestries of British life, each from their unique vantage points. Through their words, I felt as if I was walking the cobbled streets of Victorian London or attending a ball in Regency-era England. Their works did more than just improve my English; they expanded my worldview, gave depth to my understanding of British culture, and instilled a lasting love for classic literature.

While these books helped me with my English, I was regularly tying myself in knots (an English idiom, note!) with the grammar. The birds flied away or the birds flew away? One ship, two ship, or two ships? What did it mean to rain cats and dogs? What would a stitch in time achieve? It was tough but I adored the language and clung to every word my teachers and professors spoke. I found it difficult to speak up myself and suffered the embarrassment of blushes when called on. We'd had such a disciplined, quiet, regime at my boarding school and now I was expected to offer opinions and to use my voice.

Over the two years of my study, I slowly grew in confidence. It helped, too, to know that my mother and stepfather were close by and that my mother was happy. Mum had begun working for Jack Ma, who later set up the Alibaba Group and became one of the richest men in Asia. My sister, too, was doing well at work. It seemed that the early struggles we had all endured were now safely consigned to the past. My university timetable was not as intense as that of my high school, so this provided me with the opportunity to accumulate the funds required to take me to the West.

I had a few part-time jobs during the two years that I was at the university. At the weekends, I taught a bank manager's son computer skills and basic English language. Two or three evenings a week, I managed an Internet Cafe which was a fairly new thing at that time. I received some training so I was able to assist anyone who came in and correct any errors that might crop up. My computer skills were enhanced greatly. I had managed by then to learn how to build websites. Jack Ma, who rented the office building for his China Yellow Page business where my mother worked, asked if I would be interested in staying and sleeping in the building overnight from 10:00pm to 6:30am each day as a form of security for the offices. The office building was only a 15-minute walk from the university, so I took up this offer which had the bonus of saving on my university accommodation fees. In order to encourage me in my studies, Jack Ma kindly wrote to me in English a few times to boost my studies. He also gave me some clothes, which I truly appreciated. To me, Jack wasn't just a budding entrepreneur; he symbolised the dreams I had for myself. His letters, filled with hope, often uplifted me. In one, he said, "It's not where you start but where you aim. Keep learning and stay hungry." His words reflected the life he lived. Each chat with Jack was a valuable lesson in determination and foresight.

At the university, I became good friends with Shen Qunying, who was two years older than me but was in the same academic year group. In 1999, the university radio held a singing competition in English and Qunying persuaded me to enter as she had decided to take part as well. We would practise singing together then take part with our own choice of English songs. The competition was held over a period of three months and we had to sing a different song each month. My three choices were – "Nothing's Gonna Change My Love For You", "More Than I Can Say" and "Yesterday" (the famous Beatles song). Each month the students voted and some contestants would be eliminated. Qunying was very proficient at reading music and helped me to improve my singing voice as well. At the end of the competition, Qunying won and I came in the top 40 out of an entry of 1,200 students. Qunying went on to become a famous singer in China whilst I now only sing in the shower!

All the while I was planning my next steps. I was still determined to make the most of my improved English and go abroad when the time was right. On Saturdays, my friend Xia Ning and I would attend the 'English Corner' in the park, by the side of West Lake, where students gathered to speak exclusively in English. We'd always vowed to go abroad together but, when I started applying for a student visa, he shied away from the idea. I was sad that all our discussions resulted in his staying behind but I couldn't let that dampen my own desire to see the West for myself. I'd worked, and was continuing to work, so very hard to achieve this dream.

I had my first proper romantic relationship at university. It would never have been allowed at school as I'd have been expelled. We were in the same class and went to the cinema together, saw our friends and ate out at restaurants. We talked about the future, she and I, and we'd sit in the Internet Cafe, where I worked part-time in the evenings, and chat. It was a lovely, care-free time.

Yet I knew I would never stay in China – I knew my future lay elsewhere, and I didn't want to hurt her by promising something I couldn't commit to. We broke up but remained good friends afterwards. It's important to treat people with the same respect you'd wish to be treated with and I was determined to ensure that my choices would not have a detrimental effect on those I loved.

Hangzhou, with its mix of ancient beauty and flourishing economy, became more than just a city to me; it was a crucible where my aspirations, dreams, and skills were forged. Every winding alley, shimmering lakeside view and towering skyscraper became symbols of my journey from a wide-eyed newcomer to a young adult ready to take on the world. In its embrace, I was introduced to the transformative power of technology, the rich variety of classic literature and the boundless potential within myself. The bustling streets filled with students like me, all with dreams as vast as the city skyline, taught me resilience, adaptability, and the true value of perseverance.

While the magnificent West Lake reflected the tranquillity of old China, the vibrant university scene and the evolving cityscape around it embodied the pulse of a nation in rapid transition. It was in this dynamic backdrop that I realised the world was much bigger, broader and more complex than I had once imagined.

As I stood at the crossroads of tradition and modernity, Hangzhou instilled in me the courage to dream beyond borders, to embrace change, and to understand that every experience, every challenge, and every friendship was preparing me for a larger stage. And while the world beyond was vast and uncharted, my time in Hangzhou ensured that I was neither daunted nor unprepared. Instead, I was eager, ready, and equipped with the wisdom of my experiences to navigate the vast expanse of the big, wide world.

My mum and stepfather travelled to Dali in Yunnan province with my father for a holiday, photographed in 2009

CHAPTER TWELVE: WORKING NINE TO FIVE

I had completed two years of my course and was now absolutely certain that I wanted to finish my studies abroad in an English-speaking country. I had chosen to study English because it was an international language that would give me more opportunities and the advantage for a better future. However, it struck me that it might be a good idea to gain some work experience in China first. I needed to improve my English before diving in at the deep end. If I completed my four-year course in China, the likelihood would be that I'd be encouraged to become a teacher of English myself at the university.

Flattering as this was, I had observed the life of my university teachers and noted that while they were calm, intelligent people, their lives were a little too tranquil for my liking. They had been students of English here and had simply never left. Whilst I recognise I am grateful for their inspiration, I have to say I never wanted to be a teacher myself; I wanted more colour, more ups and downs, more highs and lows, and I knew that these would only be found beyond the field of education.

"What should I do, Mum?" I remember asking, when I went home one weekend. "I could stay and take up a job at Hangzhou after I've finished."

"What do you want to do?" she asked me. She knew the answer already.

It must have been difficult for my mother because her sacrifice had provided me with the choices in the first place. She had given me the courage to pursue my dreams, which could lead to my departure; from her and my sister.

"Biao," she said, smiling, "Just do whatever you think is best. You don't have to finish your course if you don't want to. If you complete it now, you may regret it forever."

I knew what I wanted, but it was reassuring to hear her unswerving support for me. Many parents might have forced me to finish. Instead, my mother refused to make the choice for me. She told me, in no uncertain terms, that I must do what I thought best.

So, in June 2000, when I was 21, I left my university course. My high school classmate, Cui Hongliang, told me that a foreign-trade company was recruiting someone who could read and write in English. I didn't feel nearly qualified enough but imagined there was no harm in applying. There was a slim chance that I would get it but if I didn't send my CV, there was absolutely no chance! I was excited to be invited for an interview in Shanghai but at the same time, I was very nervous as this was my first job interview. It was the first time I had ever worn a suit and tie, which I had borrowed from my stepfather. Shanghai is 110 miles from Hangzhou and it was a two-hour journey on the train. "I haven't completed my degree yet," I told the panel, determined to be entirely honest with them. Imagine my astonishment when, three days later, I was offered the job. What a boost for my confidence as many applicants had postgraduate or even doctorate degrees in English. When I started, I asked the manager why they employed me and he replied, "You didn't ask how much the salary was which signified the job was more important than the salary. I was very impressed and that was why you were appointed."

When I moved from the tranquil Qiuai town to bustling Hangzhou, I thought I'd seen a huge shift. But arriving in Shanghai was a whole new world. If Qiuai was a cosy hometown and Hangzhou a lively city with historical charm, Shanghai was the epitome of global vibrancy.

Everywhere I looked, skyscrapers reached for the sky, and the city's energy was palpable, day or night. During the day, streets buzzed with business folks and tourists, while nighttime unveiled a neon-lit spectacle of nightlife, markets, and an iconic riverside skyline.

Shanghai wasn't just a mix of old and new, but a melting pot of cultures, cuisines, languages, and international businesses. Everywhere, there was a sense of ambition and the city's dynamic future. Shanghai is a global city that never sleeps.

In essence, while Hangzhou felt like a melodious tune, Shanghai was a full-blown orchestra, bursting with life and surprises at every turn.

The company I joined was a successful worldwide manufacturer of air purifiers and humidifiers. In my role as an International Marketing and Promotions Executive Assistant at the company, I frequently interacted with clients from the USA, Japan, and Korea. These interactions required fluency in English and an understanding of each region's cultural etiquette. My tasks extended beyond client communication, encompassing the design and execution of marketing campaigns in collaboration with our internal team. Analysing data to gauge our marketing effectiveness was essential, as was managing our email campaigns. Occasionally, my responsibilities stretched to cater to clients' local needs or even guiding them around, showcasing the unpredictable nature of the international trading world. This position was not only demanding but also immensely educational, teaching me invaluable lessons about global marketing and sales.

All my work colleagues were very friendly and some took me to different parts of Shanghai. I was fascinated by the contrast between the Western and Chinese architecture of the city. Many of the buildings beside the Huangpu River were built by the British in the 19th Century. There was also a large French Quarter with tree-lined streets resembling Paris. Although many of the traditional Chinese houses had been replaced by large tower blocks there were still some old Chinese temples which were opened to the public.

After work, I would often go and sit on the Bund – a mile-long stretch of promenade along the Huangpu River – and watch the ships moving up and down whilst wondering about all the places they were going to and coming from. The Bund was full of tourists, both Chinese and Western. Sometimes I would be asked to take a photo by foreign visitors. They would be surprised when I started talking to them in English. I would ask them where they came from and what they thought of Shanghai. There were a few times when I offered to be their free tour guide at the weekends. This was very beneficial for me as at work I was often asked to show our clients around the city.

However, the husband and wife who ran the air purifier business constantly argued and sometimes threw things at each other in the office. One day the wife – who was in charge of the company purse-strings – came to ask me why we were spending so much money on calling abroad. I tried to explain that it was much more difficult to close deals via email; some people preferred to deal with a real human being and often there were urgent matters that needed immediate attention. "You're spending 230 Yuan RMB (£23) a month on these calls," she said crossly, waving the bill before me. "Can't you just switch to email?"

This proved to be the least of my problems. When some American clients came to Shanghai on three-to-five-day trips, they'd ask me to find them women to party with in the evenings. I felt like a pimp and became increasingly uncomfortable with these requests. On one occasion the client asked me to find a prostitute and I had no idea where to start. I called my manager who agreed to help but wanted me to stay and translate! The weight in my chest grew heavier with every word the client spoke, a knot of discomfort forming in my stomach and I realised this business wasn't right for me. I stayed for eight months and put it down to experience, but one I wasn't keen to repeat. As is so often the case in life, you have to discover what it is you definitely don't want to do, and in doing so you'll realise what works best for you. In retrospect, while the role was demanding and often required me to wear multiple hats, it provided a holistic exposure to the world of international business and was instrumental in shaping my understanding of global trade dynamics.

In February 2001, I moved to Shaoxing. It is a city between Ningbo and Hangzhou and the place where my maternal grandparents were born and grew up. I began working for a paper-printing company, who provided me with rented accommodation, which was a great bonus. Again, I was working in marketing and sales – especially international sales. Through my research I realised we could use Shaoxing's best-known resource – bamboo. Its vast forests had led to a tourism industry and bamboo was a highly useful and edible plant.

Shaoxing had a reputation for making folding-fans which sold only in China. My thought was to transform the company from a printing firm to a folding-fan business. I saw an opportunity to extend sales to other parts of the world. My boss had connections with smaller businesses and was keen to see if these could be amalgamated. I started marketing the company on the internet (the first folding-fan company in China to have a dedicated English website) and the boss was delighted when it opened up international markets. Within a few months, we saw orders coming in from the UK, Spain and the United States. The company's information was printed on the fan itself – a nifty bit of advertising that meant customers would see our brand and read about our product over and over again as they used the fan. Fans are useful not only in China, after all! This was a really good business model where an owner was open to ideas from members of his staff. My knowledge of English was a key driver here, which he put to good use. For the owner, having the right people, in the right positions, sharing ideas and working in his business, was key to success – this was embedded into my way of working later.

I returned 15 years later, on holiday with my latest colleague, Philip, who was keen to visit them after what I had shared with him about my time there. It was gratifying to see the place where I'd first seen the fruits of my labours and the sense of satisfaction it brought. Yes, I'd worked 14 hours a day for 10 months, mastering Photoshop, Dreamweaver and production processes before I handed over the reins to the boss's son. I was keen to move on but in hindsight, it had been worth it. The company had grown in size and now owned, instead of renting, its premises, which was a sure sign of success. The owner's son told me that their fans had been used as a national gift to the heads of state at the opening ceremony of the Beijing Olympic Games in 2008 and the Nanjing Summer Youth Olympic Games in 2014.

After Shaoxing, I moved back to Hangzhou and joined a firm called 21st Century Education, who recruited foreign teachers to work in China. This truly was the ideal job for someone looking to improve their English and I spoke with many prospective American teachers. I also made a good friend called Lyle from Minnesota, who came to teach and liked China so much his wife, Mary, joined him. It felt good to meet someone from a different background who took to me and China so wholeheartedly. It was interesting to hear from them about American culture. What shocked me to the core was their gun laws which allowed all Americans the right to bear arms and to use them to defend themselves.

I began to realise, too, that the grammar and pronunciation of British and American English were very different. When 21st Century Education decided to expand their business and manage students overseas, they asked me to be their agent. I did this for the Paris Management School London Campus, which became very important to me and my own story. Overseas study, particularly between China and the UK, was becoming increasingly popular at this time and a lot of British universities were coming to China to promote themselves to our students. As I helped organise and liaise at the conferences they'd attend, I recognised that this would be my future, and it filled me with joy. I was now ready to embark on my own journey to the West.

Those two years of work experience were truly invaluable in helping to build my self-confidence. I had learnt such a lot about how important social networking was in business; that good marketing improves the sales of products and that it is important a company website gives their products the best internet promotion. My initial plan had been to travel to the United States when fate intervened – as it did for so many thousands of others – on 11th September 2001, with the awful terrorist attack on the Twin Towers in New York. I had received an offer to study at the University of Buffalo and was incredibly excited about it. I had been looking at universities that both produced good results and had a good global ranking. This university had produced some well-known business entrepreneurs who had studied in the school of management there. But the climate at that time was one of fear and suspicion and I didn't relish the threat of such appalling terrorism during my first foray into the West. In view of the situation in the United States, I changed my plans and made the decision to head for England instead. And now I can say, with the benefit of hindsight, that it was indeed the best choice.

Reflecting on those two pivotal years in China, I often marvel at the serendipitous dance of life and its unexpected turns. I had delved into diverse industries, met a myriad of people, and encountered challenges that had pushed me to evolve both professionally and personally. Through it all, the rhythm of Shanghai's bustling streets, the serenity of Shaoxing's bamboo forests, and the earnest conversations along the Bund became the soundtrack to my growth.

Each experience, each misstep, each victory, served as a lesson, shaping my worldview. I had come to understand the nuances of international business, the significance of cultural respect, and the weight of ethical decisions. And while my journey had been anything but linear, the assortment of these moments painted a vibrant portrait of my young professional life.

Yet, as I stood on the precipice of another new adventure, the pull of the unknown beckoned stronger than ever. The winds of change were blowing again, carrying with them whispers of cobblestone streets, historic landmarks, and perhaps, the British accent that had always intrigued me. England awaited, and with it, a new chapter, new challenges, and promises of an even more diverse adventure ahead. The journey was far from over; in fact, it was only just beginning.

CHAPTER THIRTEEN: OFF TO ENGLAND

No one could have prepared me for life in the UK. No matter how much I'd studied and I'd learned; no matter the work experience; no matter the warm welcome I received – it was an absolute baptism of fire. To say I experienced a culture shock would be an understatement. It was a transition so severe and overwhelming it took me about six months to adjust. Despite having travelled around a fair amount during the previous two years, I'd never left China. I'd never even been further than the eastern-coastal areas where I was born, grew up, and attended university. And now, bizarrely, here I was in London. The date was 18th June 2002.

A few weeks before I left for England, I went to see my father and he announced that he had saved some money for me. However, I refused to take it as I could see that he needed it more than I did. I was grateful and touched by his offer of support. University education is expensive wherever you go in the world but especially in the UK. I had held three part-time jobs whilst at the university in

China and three full-time jobs in the two years prior to moving to the UK. I had saved £5,000 to take with me. My stepfather generously gave me another £5,000 and, as a family, we borrowed £10,000. The cost of the tuition was £6,000 so I arrived in the country with £14,000 to my name – no small sum and a good buffer in case of financial difficulty.

At Shanghai Pudong International Airport my mum, stepfather, sister and three friends saw me off. Before entering the security check gate my mother and sister gripped my hands tightly and tears fell freely from their eyes. This was the first time in my life I saw my mum cry; she had never cried in front of us when my sister and I were young. I think because she didn't want to worry us and because it was important to her to reassure us everything would be OK. Remember that Chinese people do not often express their feelings. At that moment, I hugged them with tears in my own eyes and told them not to worry and that I would be alright. I promised I would call them as soon as I arrived in the UK. It was a very strange feeling, not knowing when and where I would see them again.

Boarding an aeroplane was a novel experience in itself. Some of my peers had been to neighbouring countries, like Thailand or Japan, which were different enough from China. I had no idea what to expect of the UK even though it was somewhere I'd given so much thought to and read about so widely. I was about to find out that Dickens wasn't much use when I touched down in the busy heart of contemporary London. There were no introductory programmes, even as recently as 20 years ago, to help foreign students acclimatise to life in Britain. I knew that

I would have to be brave and try my best to adjust.

On the 12-hour flight to London, I didn't sleep at all and attempted to practise my English with the Virgin Atlantic cabin staff. I enjoyed watching a programme on the plane called "Absolutely Fabulous" and was surprised and delighted at the silliness of British humour. The mixture of excitement and nervousness lasted until I landed at Heathrow airport when the latter largely displaced the former. It was not long before I faced my first challenge.

"Do you have your recent chest x-ray medical document with you?" the immigration officer asked me.

"No sir," I replied. "I am sorry. I didn't know that I needed one."

"I am afraid you cannot enter the country without your chest x-ray medical document because China is a tuberculosis-endemic country," he said.

I didn't know what to do. The immigration officer saw that I was very concerned and said "Please wait for a moment. I'll go and check if the Medical Unit at the airport is free to x-ray you now."

Fortunately, I could have the x-ray done and it showed that I was clear of TB. I was given permission to enter the UK, which was a relief!

After leaving Passport Control, I became instantly lost. I knew what a customer was but what was "customs"? Did I have anything to declare? What did all these signs mean and why hadn't I encountered anything like them before? I began to sweat profusely, and wondered how on earth I was to survive this country if I couldn't even navigate the airport arrivals.

"Excuse me, sir, can you please let me know how I can get to Rochford in Essex?" I asked the ticket officer. He replied "You can take the Heathrow Express to London Paddington. From London Paddington Underground, you can take the tube to Liverpool Street and from there you can take a train to Rochford. Or you can take the Piccadilly Line tube from Heathrow Terminals 2 & 3 to Holborn and then switch to the Central Line to London Liverpool Street. From there you can take a train to Rochford." I was so confused because I didn't even know what the Heathrow Express or the tube was. Luckily, a lady passenger heard the conversation and offered to accompany me to the Heathrow Terminals 2 & 3 Underground station. She then helped me to buy a ticket and showed me on a map how I could get to Liverpool Street station. That was when I realised the word 'tube' means the metro system which we had in China. It took me more than four hours to get to Rochford and I was so exhausted.

Rochford is just over forty miles east of London. I lived there during my first six months in the UK. It is a small town in a quiet and rural area. It was the perfect introduction to the UK – not too busy or hectic and quaint in its habits. The university had provided me with a list of families who took in international students and I'd chosen to live with one of them, rather than student accommodation, in order to improve my spoken English and learn about British culture. I never wanted to spend all my time speaking Mandarin with other Chinese students. I might as well have stayed in Hangzhou if that's what I had wanted! I lived with an elderly couple in a house surrounded by a farm. I grew to appreciate the sleepy feel of the place and the bracing half-hour walk to the train station. From the start I found the local people incredibly friendly – they didn't often see Chinese people so they were interested in me and keen to chat.

I was like a sponge in those first months – eager to learn and drink it all in. Whatever was suggested to me, I tried. The first weeks were tough, but I wanted to learn the differences between China and the UK at first-hand, so I 'put myself out there' – to use the British expression. One day, after studying in London, I was on the train back home to Rochford and an elderly couple sitting beside me started a conversation with me, but I struggled to understand what they were saying. The only thing I could do was smile and tell them that I was new here in the UK. I felt embarrassed by my inability to understand them and my confidence took a definite knock.

I started to go out less and less because I was afraid of making a fool of myself. I decided to commit myself to my studies as much as possible. I found the professors hard to understand sometimes and would spend hours poring over my notes trying to work out what they'd meant. To help improve my understanding of spoken English I started watching British comedy programmes on the TV but I was still hesitant to talk in English. My main teacher, Ruth, was very kind and encouraged me to speak more which helped me overcome my confidence problem and slowly I began to speak more freely. I am thankful for the support she gave me, and we remain in touch to this day.

Dr Claudio Ague and his wife Rose, who I stayed with in Rochford, were a great help to me in adjusting. He was a retired psychiatrist and had worked on many criminal cases providing evidence when there was a question of diminished responsibility.

"I think you struggle slightly to express your feelings," said the doctor about a fortnight after I'd moved in.

I nodded as I knew that this was partly an aspect of my personality but also due to the cultural differences between the UK and China. We weren't raised to open up to those around us in the same way and I was determined from then onwards to adopt a more extroverted persona.

On Saturdays, I began to attend free, government-funded, English classes for foreigners. I found the information at the local library in Rochford and decided to attend in order to make some friends. I got on very well with the English teacher, Ms Aryani Lund, who was also kind enough to drive me to Rayleigh several times to have a go at playing table tennis in a local club there. After my English lesson, on my way home, I'd nod to the solitary horse in the field by the doctor's house and, over time, began to feed him apples.

"Oh dear, you really mustn't," said Rose, laughing, when she discovered I was in the habit of doing this. "The apples are too acidic – he'll get stomach problems!"

I grew to realise that the English were a lot more plain-speaking than I'd anticipated. However, that night, I didn't sleep well and worried that the horse might die the next day. The horse was fine and it survived my apples. To this day I have never poisoned an English horse, or anyone else, come to think of it!

Rose was a good cook, and I normally had dinner with her and Claudio most evenings. I never ate all the food she gave me and always left a small amount on my plate. After a few days, Rose asked me, "Biao, do you not like my cooking? You seem to be struggling to eat it all."

"No, I really enjoy eating your food. It's delicious," I told her.

"Am I giving you too much to eat as you never eat it all?" she asked.

I was a bit surprised she was asking this as, in China, when you are having a meal in someone else's house, it is polite to leave some food on your plate to show the host that their meal was filling and satisfying. I told this to Rose and she laughed and explained that, in Britain, it is polite to always finish the food on your plate – a custom which I then willingly adopted.

I commenced my Bachelor of Business Administration (BBA) studies almost immediately at the Paris Graduate School of Management and International Business at Birkbeck College's London campus. When I first stepped inside the main building, it didn't feel like a university but more like its neighbour, the British Museum. I was overcome with happiness, particularly when I saw the library. I couldn't believe the access I now had to anything I wanted to read. I went almost every day after my lectures ended. I couldn't have been more impressed with Birkbeck.

The BBA degree took me up to the following July, in 2003, and I was enrolled on its final year. It was an intense course which covered everything from advanced professional English to Business Financial Management and much in between.

My tutor, Professor Vincent, took a group of 14 international students to Brighton the month I arrived in the UK. The intention was to show us some typical British culture and scenery outside the capital. While six of us walked along the beach, we suddenly realised we'd wandered into what must have been a nudist area – you can imagine my utter shock! I'd never seen anything like it and three of my Iranian classmates turned and fled. It was another important learning curve for me when I realised that, although the stereotype of the British stiff-upper-lip held true in some regards, others of their social mores were quite the opposite to what I'd been led to believe. My good friend Rita, a classmate from Hong Kong, berated me afterwards for not bringing her along to experience this unforgettable moment!

I could see, to my relief, that my decision to live with an English host family had been the right one. Some of the international students were still clumsy and unpractised when it came to spoken English even after five years here. I was absolutely determined to continue to make myself understood and to learn when I couldn't quite fathom what a person was saying or how they meant it.

There were nine Chinese students on my course but most of them lived together and it was clear they weren't progressing nearly as quickly as they might have done had they lived apart. The same was true for my Nigerian and Iranian counterparts. Living with a host family was more nerve-wracking and certainly more solitary than an enormous shared house or dorm, but I hadn't spent all this money and worked this studiously to come to the UK and not throw myself into the language, the culture and the etiquette. My friends seemed to be learning English only in the classroom, and not in the real world. I could have done that in China! It meant I had to work a great deal harder than they did, though.

I quickly realised that referring to any group as "English" was a faux pas, given that England, Wales, Scotland and Northern Ireland are different nations. British students were very relaxed and keen to help me. It would have been a waste not to use the expertise and experience of native speakers, especially when they were so friendly and outgoing. They were very keen to hear about my life back in China and its fascinating culture.

I find it interesting, after almost 20 years in the UK, to recall my first impressions of this country. There was so much, as a young man in China, I couldn't have anticipated about the diversity and variety of this place and its people. I couldn't understand a lot of native speakers when I first moved here – particularly those from Essex, Glasgow or South Wales. The accents and dialects eluded me, as did the regionally-specific idioms and phrases. What did it mean to be told "on your bike"? When and how could something be "not my cup of tea"? Why did so many people call me "mate"? What was "taking the mickey"? Why did some British people refer to pounds and others to "quids"? What did it mean to be "quids in" anyway? I had no idea what it meant "to beat around the bush"; or how to be "knackered"; or why something was referred to as "interesting", even when it clearly wasn't! In addition, I was mortified to find "How do you do?" was a relic of the past. I longed to return to Chinese students studying English back at home and impart this knowledge. What I didn't know at the time was how expressive the English language can be. For example, there are six times as many words in the English language as there are in French. English, however, is a 'mongrel' language with roots in many others – German, French, Greek and Latin – so ideas can be expressed in many different ways. This is why the UK has produced so many writers – from Chaucer, to Shakespeare, to Bernard Shaw and many others. The language continues to grow with many of the 'new words' in the dictionary over the last fifty years hailing from the United States.

I've noticed that this is a common complaint of students from other countries about any language they're studying. The grammar, phrases and vocabulary learnt at school very often fail to capture the nuances of modern speech and native speakers are nonplussed at the old fashioned styles of language teaching. I was desperately keen to adjust to varieties of accent and expression so I could natter away just as they did.

And, boy, did the English speak fast. They spoke in rapid sentences all strung together that I found almost impossible to follow. Added to this was my growing dread of eye contact. In China, it isn't common to look someone directly in the face when you're talking to them. It felt like laser beams were trained upon me as I tried to communicate.

I'd arrived at the height of British summer (paltry in comparison to the blazing heat and humidity of Chinese summers). I was struck by the difference in the lengths of the days as autumn approached and, by December, the daylight only seemed to appear for a few hours at a time. I did, of course, notice how much the British like to talk about the weather – mainly complaints naturally – but it is a great way to 'break the ice', if you get my drift.

Socially, there were so many other shifts I'd have to grow accustomed to.

"Biao," my British friends would whisper, "You can't slurp your soup like that!"

We'd be seated at a restaurant and I, thinking I was showing appreciation for good food, was quickly introduced to the notion of silent dining without accompanying noises of satisfaction. British food I found incredibly bland and one-dimensional. It lacked the flavour and variety of Chinese cuisine. I was absolutely appalled that the British also drank their tea with milk! But now, I, of course, have been won over and enjoy a good cup of tea in the morning with milk.

Some discoveries were interesting rather than shocking. Meals were served in stages here, with a starter, main course and finally a dessert all appearing at different times. In China, it's much more common for food to appear much at the same time. I quickly discovered Chinatown, just a stone's throw from Birkbeck, and would head over to Soho to enjoy delicious, fragrant noodles with spicy beef which reminded me of home. I also found some decent barbecued chicken in Sainsbury's so, if I arrived home late, I would cook supper for myself. I sometimes missed home-cooked Chinese food and often I volunteered to cook Chinese meals for Claudio and Rose at the weekends to keep my culinary skills alive. Listen, I said to myself sternly, after a while – this cannot go on. You've got to throw yourself into British culture and that means accepting the food. Try to find the things you do like, rather than dismissing it all. This process of talking to myself and ensuring I didn't resist the culture shock was as important outside the kitchen or restaurant as inside it.

Although we'd been exposed to the more extroverted, less conservative, side of the country's culture on the beach at Brighton, I soon became aware of the ingrained politeness of the majority of people I met. There were a lot of "pleases and thank yous", "sorrys and excuse mes". In China if you hold the door open for someone people will usually walk straight through it without saying a word. It isn't considered rude – it's just how things are done. I also realised that people didn't speak loudly in public and, when they did speak, men mostly talked about the weather, football, cricket and rugby. But British people seemed a lot more willing to discuss how they were feeling which I wasn't used to and took some time to feel comfortable with. I found everyone gentle and polite, fairly conservative, but always ready to help.

I also realised the way people greet each other in the UK is very different to how it is done in China. In the UK, people greet each other with

"Hello, how are you?" but don't expect to get a reply about how you are. In China, it is normal to greet someone with

"Hello, have you eaten?" or "Hello, you have put on some weight."

In the UK, to tell someone they have put on weight can be taken as an insult but, in China, it is taken as a compliment. It means you are well off and not doing hard physical labour.

Similarly, just as customs about commenting on someone's weight differ, so do traditions related to entering someone's home. In China, our shoes are more than just protective footgear; they're carriers of the dust and stories from the roads we've travelled. It's a shared understanding that when you step into a home, you leave your shoes and the outside world at the entrance. The custom is as much about cleanliness as it is about respect for the sanctity of someone's abode.

In contrast, the UK, while having its quirks, doesn't follow the universal Chinese 'shoes-off' policy. It's not unusual to walk through homes with shoes on, tracing steps across plush carpets and polished wooden floors. Exceptions are made for muddied boots or rain-soaked shoes, of course, but on the whole, the British are more relaxed about indoor footwear.

So there I was, invited into a quintessential British home, instinctively slipping off my shoes like a programmed robot. The puzzled look from my host was a gentle reminder that I wasn't in China any more. They handed my shoes back, chuckling, "We don't mind shoes indoors; just not the muddy ones!"

It was a small, humorous lesson in cultural nuances. Two countries, thousands of miles apart, with simple differing views on shoes – and a world of stories between them.

Beyond my experiences in Britain, the University offered us opportunities to explore further afield, including a three-day field trip to Paris along with nine classmates. Most of them went off to Disneyland but Rita, Jinjin and I stayed in the city centre by ourselves. We were delighted with the opportunity to roam at will. Jinjin was the same age as me and she came from Shanghai. The three of us used to study and have lunch together at the University so, when we arrived in Paris, we volunteered to share a room together. We went to Notre Dame, the Louvre, and boarded a boat for a cruise down the Seine. As the sun started to sink and, with no smartphones to help us, we soon realised we were hopelessly lost.

"Excuse me," we asked the locals rushing past. "Could you possibly help us? We're lost!"

"I don't speak English," came the inevitable reply in English.

Eventually, we managed to make our way back to our hotel in a taxi. Drama over! Despite this hiccup, it felt wonderful to be seeing how life was lived over the Channel. Paris was memorable not just for its landmarks, but for the bond I built with two of my classmates.

After we graduated, Rita returned to Hong Kong and became a purchasing manager in an electronic company. Jinjin is now a fortune teller in Shanghai. We still keep in touch.

Leaving China behind had been a wrench for many reasons but one of the biggest was the long-held, cherished memories of my care-free childhood in the mountains and the abundance of nature to be found there. Imagine my surprise and delight, then, when I found that the UK was not so different. Horses, rabbits, deer, hedgehogs, squirrels and badgers that had made their home here were fascinating, as were the different species of birds, from seagulls to robins, and – the most common in London – pigeons. I'd walk through the city on weekends and notice foxes skulking away in the early morning, a flash of orange whipping out of sight behind the bins. The shops and public services, I found, were often closed at the weekends, or operated with limited hours. In China, they were always open seven days a week. But this didn't matter much to me. However, I found life in the UK incredibly expensive compared to life back home.

One of the most shocking differences was the shortness of the British school day. Children walking down the streets at 3.30pm were finished for the day! It seemed amazing that they should have so much free time to themselves. This culture of individualism was extended to my own education. For the first time, I was encouraged to develop my own opinions on the reading materials and not just copy them down or learn them off by heart. At first, I found this very challenging because it was so alien to the way I'd been taught. Public presentations, to the rest of the class, for example, would see me break out in a sweat to rival that which I had experienced at Heathrow. With time the sense of terror diminished, and the new way of learning stood me in good stead further down the line so I'm grateful for it now.

Most importantly, I can now 'hold my own' when with my British friends and have a keen sense of British humour. Without 'beating around the bush', I am more than capable of 'taking the mickey', even when certain folk are 'not my cup of tea' – thank you, mates.

Navigating the cultural crossroads between China and the UK has been a journey of delightful surprises, comical misunderstandings, and heart-warming connections. As I've come to embrace the quirks of British life, I've also come to appreciate the diverse array of traditions I bring from my homeland. In the blend of the old and the new, the East and the West, I've found a harmonious balance that enriches my experience every day. England, with its peculiarities and charm, has become a second home, where I continually learn, adapt, and cherish the blend of two worlds converging. And so, amidst the tea and dim sum, I carry forth my story, eager for the chapters yet to unfold.

CHAPTER FOURTEEN: BARRY AND BRYON

There is no doubt that the friends I made here in the UK proved a real turning point for me, in more ways than one. This chapter is devoted to how I met them.

On my first week in the UK, I needed to open a bank account. Having done some research on student bank accounts, I decided to open an account with the NatWest bank on Regent Street in London. When I entered the bank and I immediately headed towards the counter. To my surprise, a polite yet stern voice interrupted my progress, "Excuse me, the end of the queue is back there." I turned around, only to realise that what I had mistaken for a group of people idly chatting was actually a perfectly formed queue, complete with subtle markers and unspoken rules!

Embarrassed, I took my place at the end. As I waited, I couldn't help but strike up a conversation with the gentleman in front of me. "In China," I laughed, "our queues aren't so... orderly. It's more of a 'push your way to the counter' system. I never imagined I'd need queue training!"

The man chuckled, "Ah, the British queue! A dance of patience, precision, and utmost politeness. You'll get the hang of it."

I was eager to practise my English and continued to chat with him as we slowly moved forward in the queue. His name was Barry Draper and he was a civil servant with business expertise. Little did I know at the time how fortuitous and important that conversation would be. We chatted for a long time then swapped details and agreed to keep in touch. It was lovely to feel that I'd been able to practise my English with a native speaker but, more importantly, that we'd made a connection. It gave me an enormous sense of pride to think that I could not only get by in English but make friends at the same time. However, I also learnt that British people do like to keep an orderly queue and frown upon those who try to cut in.

I was just a few weeks away from completing my BBA and had started researching alternative universities at which to study for my MBA which would give me the skills, knowledge and confidence to set up my own business or, at the very least, get a job in the UK. Back in 2003, the University of Luton – as it was then called – offered an MBA in International Business for £9,000. This was less than the upwards of £20,000 the London universities were charging. I attended an open day which impressed me enough to apply and I was accepted. Barry and I had been in contact by phone and email and had met when he came to London on business so we had formed a good, strong friendship. He happened to live close to the new university, in Dunstable, and, when I told him that I was looking for a place to stay in Luton, he very kindly offered to let me stay with him as a lodger until I completed my studies. Barry worked as a civil servant in Luton so could also drive me to the campus each day. Barry not only provided accommodation in his spare room but also helped me with my studies. He would often help to explain things I was struggling with. This help was further extended when the time arrived for me to write my dissertation, as he made sure I wrote correct English.

It's the stuff that dreams are made of, I think. By virtue of having been in the right place at the right time, I made a lifelong friend and met the person who would eventually become my business partner. If I'd decided to have a coffee before going to the bank that day, I'd never have met Barry. Speaking a new language is an exhausting process and on the day I met Barry, I might have felt too tired to strike up a conversation, or I might have decided to read a book while I waited, or listen to music, or a thousand other things rather than diving in and beginning to chat with a stranger. In the years to come Barry provided me with valuable assistance when he accompanied me on around 10 trips to China.

Barry was an embodiment of the classic English gentleman. With an average height, salt-and-pepper hair, and deep-set eyes, always alert, he emanated a unique blend of wisdom and playfulness. Those eyes, observant and insightful, seemed to miss nothing, but always sparkled with a warmth that drew people to him.

Away from his professional commitments as a civil servant, Barry was engaged in the film industry, working as an extra. He was also a devoted fan of football. A lifelong supporter of Luton Football Club, weekends often found him cheering passionately for his team, a ritual he held close to his heart. But football wasn't his sole sporting love. Barry had a deep appreciation for cricket. He fondly recalled his days as a player for the Eversholt Cricket Club, where he played for over a decade, immersing himself in the rhythm and nuances of the sport.

When not engrossed in sports, Barry could be found delving into the pages of a book, especially those on history. His bookshelf at home was a testament to his passion, laden with volumes that spanned eras and continents. His keen interest in history wasn't just limited to reading; he was also known to share intriguing anecdotes from the past, often peppered with his unique brand of humour.

Ah, humour! Barry had an unparalleled knack for it. His jokes, always timely and delivered with a straight face, would often catch listeners off guard, resulting in hearty laughter. His sense of humour made him popular at gatherings, making even a mundane tale unforgettable with his comedic twist.

Among his many quirks, Barry's intentional choice to wear mismatched socks was particularly endearing. When questioned, he'd respond with a chuckle, "Keeps people on their toes, doesn't it?" This trait beautifully encapsulated his approach to life: finding humour in the ordinary and cherishing life's little eccentricities.

Barry's strong belief in the importance of education, coupled with his caring manner, whether explaining a complex historical event or sharing insights from his myriad experiences, made him an invaluable mentor and guide. His essence was a harmonious blend of wisdom, humour, and a passion for life's diverse offerings.

In Barry Draper, I didn't just find a friend or mentor, but a wellspring of experience, knowledge, laughter, and genuine warmth.

While staying at Barry's, in order to practise my English and earn some money I took a job as a waiter in a Chinese restaurant in Dunstable. As an overseas student I was allowed to work up to 20 hours per week. I enjoyed meeting and talking with the customers. The tips we were given would be put in a tip box, but I was surprised and disappointed that I was never given a share. After two weeks I was told to wash dishes in the kitchen. I told the owner this was not in my job description, but he told me that it was just temporary. I missed talking to the customers and being able to practise my English. Unfortunately, three weeks later, I was still working in the kitchen, and decided to find another job.

In 2003, I also met Bryon Sawyer, through Barry, at a Christmas party. Bryon also lived in Luton. We got on very well and, when Barry retired, Bryon very kindly let me stay in his spare room. Bryon helped me with my spoken English and my understanding of British culture. Along with our mutual friend Chris Canfield, he taught me to drive and supported me when I set up my business. One of the best gifts Bryon gave me was the encouragement I needed to start playing table tennis again – something I'd always enjoyed at primary school in China.

Bryon was the antithesis of Barry in many ways. While Barry was more reserved, Bryon was the life of the party. A retired electrical engineer, he had a keen eye for detail which was evident not just in his profession but also in his hobbies. He had a miniature train set in his attic, a project he started in his early 30s, recreating scenes from different eras with meticulous precision.

Bryon cherished British traditions. Every evening, like clockwork, he would brew a pot of Earl Grey tea, insisting on using loose leaves rather than tea bags. "There's an art to it," he'd often say. His love for cooking was renowned among our friends. His speciality was the traditional British roast, but he always added a twist, like a unique herb from his window boxes.

He valued authenticity and had an infectious enthusiasm for life. It was Bryon who, on noticing my hesitancy at a karaoke night, nudged me to take to the stage and sing, saying, "Life's too short for missed opportunities."

One of his most endearing habits was writing postcards. In the age of emails and instant messaging, Bryon would send postcards from wherever he travelled, even if it was just a neighbouring town, always with a funny anecdote or observation.

Bryon treated me like his own son. He gave me insights into British traditions which acclimatised me to the UK. He was already in his late sixties when we met so it was also useful for me to see the differences in the ways that younger and older people acted and spoke in the UK. He was an excellent cook to boot and I can remember how surprised I was the first time he warmed our plates before we ate hot food.

Of all the things I'm grateful to Bryon for, and there are many, his ability to inspire confidence in me, professionally, ranks highly. I was so nervous after starting my own business, but meetings with clients were particularly nerve-wracking. I knew the topic inside out, had done my research and knew what I needed to impart, but getting the words out in a coherent way proved a real challenge. I'd practise in front of Bryon, who'd nod and tell me how to move my hands, how to stand, how to pause for breath and maintain eye contact with my audience. It was completely revolutionary to me and the first time I spoke publicly at the Bedfordshire Chamber of Commerce Bryon was right there supporting me in the front row. There were 24 people in attendance, a situation which would have caused me panic in the past but, thanks to Bryon's help, it was a success. I quickly realised that many of these business people were older than me, but I could use this to my advantage. I made jokes about my youthful appearance and told them that remembering how to pronounce my name was simple. "It rhymes with the noise a cat makes – just think of 'miaow'." An English friend confided in me that he still says 'miaow' in his mind before saying my name.

Bryon focussed on three main areas: encouragement, first impressions and appearance. He accompanied me, at his own request, on numerous business trips abroad. In 2006 we went to China and he asked if we could go to the village where I was born. We spent time with some members of the village, including children, who came out to greet us warmly. I have a picture that shows Bryon playing badminton with them in the same place where my friends and I used to play when we were children. This brought back many happy memories for me. We also took the opportunity of visiting my father's house where Bryon was totally fascinated by the way the bamboo chairs that he saw there were made. He later told me how much he appreciated seeing where I grew up as a child. The next visit to China, in 2009, was to an international conference hosted by the Ningbo Government. I had been asked to speak to delegates from 18 countries to promote the fashion business between them and China. This conference was held around a very large oval table and at one point my microphone stopped working. Bryon, two seats away, calmly got up and swapped his microphone with mine then returned to his seat to continue taking photographs of the proceedings.

2010 was a busy year. Bryon came with me to a conference in Malta hosted by the EU on 'Understanding China'. I was giving the keynote speech and received the following commendation from the chairperson of the conference:

I can highly recommend Biao. He has given lectures at our Chamber, especially with regards to the Chinese culture and business ethics and also helped us to establish networking and business contacts. He is highly trustworthy and efficient. Ms Helga Ellul, The Malta Chamber of Commerce Enterprise and Industry, President, Malta.

In the same year we were invited to Croatia to do another presentation about business with China, at which Bryon and Barry met the Croatian State Minister. On all of the trips, when Bryon and/or Barry accompanied me, they would always take a prominent seat on the front row so that they could have direct eye contact with me, which I found so reassuring. I am forever indebted to Bryon and Barry for helping me make a good impression on my trips abroad.

CHAPTER FIFTEEN: LIGHTNING BOLTS

In a life's journey, there are moments that define us; decisions that redirect our paths and challenges that refine our character. This chapter captures one such pivotal period in my life – a juncture where academia intertwined with real-world insights; where my Eastern roots met Western perspectives and where each lightning bolt of realisation propelled me towards my destiny. Here, amidst the historic walls of Putteridge Bury, I not only pursued an MBA but also embarked on a journey of profound personal and professional transformation.

My MBA at the University of Luton, now called the University of Bedfordshire, lasted from September 2003 until November 2004. It felt wonderful to mix with classmates from such a variety of countries and learn how to work together. We completed our studies in the idyllic surroundings of Putteridge Bury on the edge of Luton. It was open and leafy, green and calm.

Putteridge Bury wasn't just a location for my academic pursuits; it was a living testament to history, culture, and change. As I strolled through its verdant grounds, I would often reflect on the weight of the legacy that surrounded me. Every corner of this magnificent estate, with a history that predates even the Domesday Book of 1086, resonated with tales of eras gone by. I couldn't help but think of the countless souls who had trodden on the same ground, and the myriad of stories they held. The magnificent building, mirroring Chequers in its grandeur, and the tree planted by royalty, were constant reminders of the blend of history and modernity. This tableau of the past constantly served as an inspiration, urging me to bridge the old with the new in my studies. The rich backdrop of Putteridge Bury didn't just frame my academic journey, it enriched it, compelling me to think deeper, strive harder, and connect my contemporary learnings with the lessons of the past.

The MBA was demanding and included courses on financial decision-making, management information for decision-making, managing in the global environment, marketing and the environment, financial markets, international-trade relations, research methods, strategic analysis, strategic marketing and the global environment.

Among the myriad courses I embarked upon, one that particularly captured my interest was the exploration into the distinct buying behaviours between China and the West. One striking difference I came to understand was the profound emphasis the Chinese place on trust and relationship-building, or 'Guanxi', in their business dealings. While Western consumers often prioritise efficiency and directness, many Chinese consumers value the time and effort dedicated to forging a personal connection, considering it a significant factor in their purchasing decisions. This cultural nuance illuminated the intricacies of global business for me.

On the other hand, while the module on financial decision-making whilst undoubtedly important, I found somewhat less engaging. This was not due to the content itself but rather its delivery. It often felt detached from real-world business scenarios, making it challenging to connect theoretical financial models with their practical applications in dynamic business landscapes.

I also undertook a great many workshops and training courses. From Knowledge Hub and The Knowledge Network to Young Enterprise, I learnt about the basics of building a business and 'aerodynamic' email marketing. These would prove to be invaluable when I came to set up on my own.

My language skills greatly improved. I had gained valuable practice with Barry and Bryon and could now combine the best of my own culture with the best of my learned, adopted western model. Yes, they were different, these cultures – sometimes hugely so – but they were also symbiotic. They had much to teach each other. I was also starting to improve my interpersonal skills, and my sense of individual creativity and motivation. Above all, the course allowed me to develop my own planning strategies, organisational and team-management skills – all of which would prove vital for my next steps.

One of our tutors was proving most challenging to understand because he spoke quietly and indistinctly in a very large classroom. I also struggled with his accent. I barely learnt a thing and most of my peers claimed the same. I was concerned that if I raised this issue the teacher would take against me, and this was just a worry I'd have to bear. By October 2003 I felt confident enough to use my voice.

I agreed to write on behalf of the Chinese cohort to Rosemary, the dean of the student body. I explained that we were all having trouble understanding the lecturer. That English was not his first language (nor was it ours) which led to a lack of clarity. He also spoke incredibly quickly and in a monotone so much of what he said during two-hour seminars was inaudible.

Contrary to my fears, the university did swap our lecturers and Rosemary assured me that I had done the right thing. It would have seemed unthinkable just a few years before to consider writing the letter, but I knew that we could not continue to make progress without action and was proud I was able to use my written English skills to ensure change. This experience was pivotal in my understanding of the value of open dialogue, especially in a foreign environment. It underscored the significance of using one's voice for positive change, and it reinforced my belief in the power of collective action. Looking back, I realise that confronting this challenge head-on was instrumental in shaping my ability to navigate cross-cultural communication barriers and foster an environment conducive to learning and mutual understanding.

The MBA threw up various challenges. One piece of work required groups of five to undertake an assignment. Two of our group weren't really engaged with us, so they were removed. However, this meant that the three of us had to work much harder and longer to meet the deadline. There were nights when I had my doubts, questioning our ability to meet the looming deadline and produce quality work. But amidst these challenges, there were also moments of profound breakthrough. There was an evening, I distinctly remember, when, after hours of brainstorming, the pieces of our assignment began to align seamlessly. Despite occasional differences we worked well together and the project was completed successfully. The professor praised our achievements – much to our delight. This experience taught me the importance when working in a team of playing to each of the member's strengths where possible. Taking on the group project with the sudden absence of two members was nothing short of daunting. This project, more than anything, became a testament to our tenacity and willpower. The highs and lows we weathered together fostered not only professional growth but also deepened our bonds as teammates. It served as a stark reminder that while adversity can be intimidating, facing it head-on with a committed group can transform challenges into rewarding learning experiences

Handing in my dissertation concluded sixteen years of education, from primary school at Fangshuicun village in Ningbo to the last year at Putteridge Bury in Bedfordshire. Three months before completing my MBA, my two good American friends, Lyle and Mary, invited me to travel with them round Europe as part of their 50th wedding anniversary celebration and return before my graduation ceremony. It was my first visit to Belgium, Holland, Germany, Denmark and Sweden – each with their different cultures and approach to visitors – some more forthright, open and 'to the point' than others! It was useful that in each country some people spoke English.

The end of my MBA also marked another important

milestone. My mother and stepfather came to the UK for the first time to attend my graduation ceremony which made them terribly proud. I was very grateful that Barry kindly offered his home to my parents during their stay and took them to visit a number of different places in England.

"I'd like to treat them," my friend Chris Canfield said, in the days before their arrival. "Do something really special for them. They've never been here, after all."

That something special turned out to be a flight in a private helicopter, belonging to an acquaintance, which flew us to a field near Stonehenge. It was a wonderful experience and one I was humbled to share with my mum and stepfather. They also immensely enjoyed a drive through the Lake District with Bryon. It meant they were able to see a little more of the country and spend time with one of my closest friends. I had been terribly homesick during my first few months in the UK and knew that my mother and stepfather had worried about me alone in a new country. But I always told myself to stay positive, keep going and keep my chin up (to use the British expression!). My mother and stepfather said they were very proud of what I had achieved. It was also a comfort for me that they no longer had to worry about how I was coping in the UK.

I remember when my mother and stepfather stepped onto British soil for the first time, I could see a mix of excitement and apprehension in their eyes. The unfamiliar surroundings, the cool English air, and the flurry of foreign tongues were undoubtedly overwhelming. Their initial cultural shocks were both humorous and enlightening; the idea of queuing for almost everything was alien to them, and their fascination with the traditional English breakfast, with its baked beans and black pudding, led to many animated discussions at the dining table.

As they journeyed through England with Barry and Bryon, they encountered nuances of the Western world that often left them pleasantly surprised but occasionally perplexed. I remember my mother's amusement at the British politeness, often remarking, 'They say sorry even when it's not their fault!'

But more than the cultural observations, it was the shared experiences and stories exchanged between Barry, Bryon, my mother and stepfather that left an indelible mark on me. Watching my mother and stepfather converse with Barry over tea, with Bryon narrating tales of his adventures, was heart-warming. They would often navigate the language barrier with a mix of broken English, hand gestures, and a lot of laughter.

These interactions underscored a vital lesson for me. While cultural differences can be vast and sometimes challenging, human connections transcend them. The laughter, the shared meals, the stories told and heard – they all highlighted the universal human desire for understanding and connection. This visit reinforced my belief that bridging cultural gaps was not just about understanding traditions or customs, but more about forging genuine human relationships.

The research for the dissertation had included using libraries, internet searches and interviews with some businesses in the UK and China. I came to realise that most UK-China joint-business ventures fail. Generally, this could be attributed to the cultural differences in ways of working, managerial styles and expectations. There was a gap in the market in this respect and, with ever-increasing business to be done between the two countries, this was a gap I hoped to fill with some chance of success.

A good example was the closing of the Barbie doll store in Shanghai, which had been painted pink all over. To the Chinese this gave the impression it was a brothel so parents were reluctant to take their children into the store. Another example was that of Home Depot, an American DIY chain, which also failed in China. They didn't understand that nowadays most Chinese do not like to do DIY. So, although many people came into their stores, not many people bought anything once they realised they would have to fit it themselves.

While the failures of the Barbie doll store in Shanghai and Home Depot's misadventures in China might seem like cautionary tales of cultural misunderstandings, they also underscore a more profound and often overlooked aspect of international business. Truly understanding a culture is not merely a defensive strategy to sidestep pitfalls; it is a proactive approach that can unveil immense opportunities.

Take, for instance, the Barbie doll store debacle. Beyond the immediate misinterpretation of the store's appearance, there lay a deeper cultural lesson. If the store's planners had genuinely engaged with the nuances of Chinese family values, childhood aspirations, and parental concerns, they might have envisioned a completely different and more successful store concept. Perhaps an interactive play space where children could learn and grow, aligning more with Chinese parents' emphasis on education and holistic development.

Similarly, with Home Depot, the DIY culture is rooted deeply in the Western ideals of individualism and self-reliance. In China, where communal values often take precedence and where rapid urbanisation has distanced many from hands-on craftsmanship, the DIY concept didn't resonate. However, imagine if Home Depot had approached the market with a service-oriented model, offering not just products but complete home solutions, tapping into the Chinese appreciation for convenience and expertise.

These examples illustrate that true cultural understanding opens doors to innovation. It allows businesses to not just adapt their existing models, but to reimagine them, to find untapped needs and desires in a new market and to create solutions that resonate deeply. In essence, it's not just about avoiding blunders but about crafting success stories that are in tune with the heartbeat of a culture.

From my research, I realised that British business already invested heavily in China and vice-versa; but nevertheless, there were a lot of other joint ventures just waiting to be set up. British businesses knew that China was the fastest-growing economy in the world, and that Chinese businesses were growing increasingly wealthy. However, without a good understanding of how and why people work, it is difficult to succeed in business in another country.

The experience of successfully completing my MBA had given me new confidence and I now felt ready to take my next step in setting up my own business here in the UK. My professor told me that I was the first of his students to use their dissertation as the basis for a business plan. It centred on factors that influenced the success, or otherwise, of a marketing strategy and how to develop one for a small but international company.

As I reflect on my transformative journey, the concept of the 'three lightning bolts' stands as a testament to the defining moments that shaped my trajectory. Each bolt was not just a flash of inspiration but a profound realisation that guided my decisions and ambitions:

1. The Pursuit of Knowledge: My decision to embark on an MBA was the initial spark. It represented my hunger for understanding, for skills, and for bridging the East and West through education.

2. Dissertation as a Compass: Choosing my dissertation topic was more than an academic endeavour. It became the blueprint for my entrepreneurial vision, highlighting the complexities and opportunities of international business dynamics.

3. Bridging the Business Divide: Recognising the challenges UK and China businesses faced when trying to collaborate was the final bolt. It highlighted a gap in the market, an opportunity, and underscored the vital importance of cultural understanding in global business.

These bolts were not just moments of insight; they were the catalysts that propelled me forward, illuminating my path and solidifying my resolve. As they say, things come in threes, and in my journey, these three moments have been the beacons guiding me towards a future filled with potential and promise.

CHAPTER SIXTEEN: ONWARDS AND UPWARDS

I started my first venture in January 2005, Camellia Universal Limited – a China/UK business consultancy – with Chris Canfield as my business partner. He was a local councillor and the Mayor of Harpenden. He was also a school governor who had set up a government Young Enterprise scheme which was about young people starting up a business. With his business background, Chris was the ideal business partner and it felt reassuring to know I wasn't entirely alone. Looking back on the decision now it was indeed a brave one. I've since realised that, with consultancy, you need knowledge, social media for marketing and promotional skills and confidence rather than money. Money will come, but it isn't a prerequisite. So often, young entrepreneurs seem to think that an enormous pile of savings will prove the difference between early success and failure, but this prevents them having the confidence to take a punt, to have a go and see what happens. With Chris's support, and encouragement from Barry and Bryon, I took the risk of using the little money I did have and trying to grow it. In business, confidence is key. It doesn't necessarily matter how much you have in your pocket.

In those days in England, no one was allowed to set up a limited company on their own. You had to have at least one director and a company secretary. I became the director, with Chris as the company secretary. In December of 2005, he resigned and returned to politics to take up the Liberal mayoral candidacy again and Barry stepped in as company secretary – a position he holds to this day.

I told my parents that I might want to stay in the UK as it wouldn't have been fair or kind to hide such intentions from them. Although they accepted my choice, they were very surprised at my decision to set up a business on my own rather than take a salaried position at a management consultancy. In China, it is difficult enough, but in the UK – with the added barrier of language differences – it must have seemed an incredibly risky and dangerous proposition. I told them that I had a lot of support from friends and tutors. I knew that if I had a problem they would always help me.

"Don't worry, Mum," I told my mother down the phone. "It'll be OK. I'll make it work."

Consulting on business between the UK and China came quite naturally to me. I'd learned so much from my MBA – and not just academically. I'd developed good presentation and interpersonal skills whilst working on group assignments with contemporaries from countries like Pakistan, Brazil, the United States, Barbados, Iran and India. It truly was the making of me and I felt strongly that it was the springboard to the rest of my life. For each project I work on, even today, I use techniques from the business plan analysis workshops we did on my MBA course.

The aim of Camellia Universal Limited was to facilitate trade and investment opportunities between Chinese and UK businesses. We chose the name Camellia Universal as the city flower of Ningbo is in fact the Camellia, so both myself and Chris felt it was a very apt and suitable name for us. But after a while, it became clear that some people were assuming we were a florist or maybe a flower farm and someone even enquired if we needed seed money! I was subsequently told by a friend that they were in fact 'taking the Mickey' – a phrase which, of course, at the time I failed to understand totally, and assumed they were referring to the famous Disney mouse in some way!. Finally, the penny dropped another phrase I would not have used at that time, for obvious reasons – and I realised that we should probably consider changing the name to reflect better the nature of the business.

We chose Buckingham Wealth in March 2013 for a number of reasons. We felt it sounded quite 'regal', which we liked. It also fitted in well with where I was living, close to the Buckinghamshire border and not far from the town of Buckingham. And also B and W were my initials too! One of the other important factors in selecting the company's name was how it sounded to our prospective Chinese clients. In China, western words can be associated with the meanings of similar sounding Chinese words. For example, if a western company name starts with the syllable 'sir' then this would come across poorly in China as the sound 'sir' means death in Mandarin. However, the way the Chinese pronounce Buckingham resembles the words for 'white gold' in Mandarin, which obviously has all sorts of good connotations, and therefore makes it sound like a good company to do business with. So taking all of the above into consideration, we felt that Buckingham Wealth was a winning name on many fronts and decided to go with it.

When we started the business, we decided that using social media would be the most effective and efficient way to promote our business. It was a steep learning curve for me to understand how to use the different social media platforms such as LinkedIn, Facebook, Twitter, Google Blogger, Instagram and later TikTok to publicise the business and help to generate suitable leads and opportunities.

You know the saying, "Expect the unexpected"? Well, our maiden voyage into the world of business enquiries proved just that. In the early days, a London firm sent us an enquiry that truly made us raise an eyebrow. They wanted us to find a Chinese production company to craft... well, adult toys. Not exactly the sophisticated business venture I had imagined setting sail with! As I scratched my head, pondering the diverse ways entrepreneurship can surprise you, we kindly informed them of our non-speciality in that, uh, "particular" sector. This amusing request shone a light on one thing: our online advertising was a tad too ambiguous. Time to recalibrate, unless we fancied more such "stimulating" offers!

In the formative decade of our operations, our primary emphasis was on guiding British enterprises. We sought to demystify the intricate world of Chinese business, shedding light on its unique characteristics, cultural nuances and operational dynamics. Our aim was to bridge the East-West divide, enabling UK firms to effectively navigate and thrive within the vast Chinese market landscape. However, the tides of global economics began to shift. Over the last five years, with China's meteoric rise to the position of the world's second-largest economy, our focus has evolved. We have witnessed an increasing number of Chinese companies eager to make their mark in the UK. Consequently, our role has transformed from being just advisors to British firms in China, to also aiding and facilitating Chinese enterprises looking to invest and establish their foothold on British shores.

I was asked to lead a training session on Chinese business culture for Hydrogen Energy International Ltd, a joint venture between BP and Rio Tinto. They retained me as their consultant on an environmentally friendly project with the Chinese government but weren't sure how to negotiate. The one-day training programme was given to 20 people from all around the world. I asked, out of curiosity, why we, as a small company, had been chosen. They thought our social media presence was very professional, which pleased me after all the time we had put into it. Afterwards, I was delighted to receive a letter of recommendation:

The seminar 'Doing Business in China – Know the Game' was very useful and appropriate for our need. Carlos Barrera, Hydrogen Energy International Ltd – a joint venture between BP & Rio Tinto, UK

In 2009, I was commissioned by Delphi Automotive Systems, who are a vehicle components manufacturing company in Luton, England, to help them prepare for a potential takeover by a Chinese business, Beijing West Industry (BWI). My remit was to deliver a training programme to the management team, so they could fully comprehend the major differences between their usual way of conducting business, and the corresponding Chinese business and social cultural norms. After due preparation and the appropriate transfer of knowledge, everything was in place for when the Chinese delegates arrived.

In order to welcome the Chinese investment delegation, the Delphi team arranged for them to experience a traditional British fine dining meal at one of the UK's oldest restaurants in the nearby village of Ivinghoe.

The Chinese delegation brought a bottle of strong Chinese white liquor, with an alcohol content of 53%, to the restaurant, along with some fine Scottish whisky, an export product not usually available in the UK. Fortunately, my training to the Delphi team had covered the tendency of some Chinese business leaders to take their favoured drinks to restaurants, and they had therefore been able to forewarn the maître d' and ensure that this would not cause any issues. While we were still at the dining table, the head of the delegation poured some white liquor into everybody's glass, lifted his glass and said "bottoms up". The strong white liquor was then swiftly followed by the Scottish whisky.

However, this presented me with a specific problem. Being very aware of my limitations when it came to strong liquor, I found myself with a tricky real-time operational decision to make. The choices were as follows:

1st choice: if I were to refuse to drink the Chinese white liquor and whisky, there was a high risk that I might offend the Chinese investment delegation and they might not go ahead with the deal.

2nd choice: if I were to decline the drink with a specific and reasonable explanation, then although I might not offend the visiting delegation, there was a real risk that I could fail to build the necessary rapport and relationship with them because in the north part of China, drinking alcohol together during the meal is a very important cultural element of relationship building.

3rd choice: drink and hope against hope that I would still be able to retain the ability to act appropriately in the role of intermediary even while under the influence. After all, surely there was a chance that I would not get drunk at all and everything would be fine? Surely...?

I decided to go with choice number 3. My client had arranged transport for me both to and from the restaurant which made me feel better. He also had the experience of working with Japanese businessmen and had learnt from my training that Chinese business manners are quite different to traditional British business etiquette! So I knew he would understand my difficulty. I must admit that choice 3 did lead to me getting a little drunk, but in my defence, this was in no small way due to the head of the Chinese delegation realising my pretty low alcohol tolerance, and subsequently having a little good natured fun at my expense.

The next day was, thankfully, a non-working day for me,

and my client telephoned me during the day to confirm that the negotiation was progressing well. He did laugh at my suffering of the previous day and reminded me that it was all in a good cause! The deal was successfully agreed at a later date.

Whatever I felt at the time, I concluded that I must have done a good job because I was subsequently employed again... but never allowed to forget my inebriation!

Since 2005 I have had many occasions to travel to China on business but also to take the opportunity to see my family. This was a major influence behind my decision to focus on this specific type of consultancy.

In 2006, I saw a BBC news clip about Savile Row in London's West End which, for two centuries, has been leading the world in men's bespoke tailoring. It reported that the companies could not attract young apprentices into the profession whilst the current master tailors were ageing. Rising rents and rates were proving costly to the tailoring trade. There was an urgent need to attract the young people into the profession otherwise handcrafted tailoring could die out.

I hadn't heard of Savile Row and knew nothing of its history as a historic street in Mayfair, central London, famous as the home of traditional men's bespoke tailoring. It is a name synonymous with masculine elegance, time-honoured tradition and discreet luxury. For almost five hundred years, this quiet and civilised street has played host to generations of the most talented artisans, meticulously dressing gentlemen and ladies, of taste in some of the finest bespoke garments in the world.

I realised there was an opportunity here, but where to start?

Britain occupied Ningbo in 1842, under the treaty of Nanjing. Many wealthy British and other Europeans settled in there and Shanghai. They brought their master tailors with them to provide the comforts of home. They also recruited Chinese dressmakers as well as the sons of farmers. The small hands of these young farm boys were well-suited to the craft and they seized the opportunity to escape the hard agricultural life at home.

In 1928, at the height of Shanghai's Grand Days – when it was known as "The Paris of the East, the New York of the West" – practically all the tailors in Shanghai were Chinese. It was during this time that Ningbo-born tailors acquired an international reputation for being world-class. They were known as 'Hongbang Cai Feng', or 'Red Group Tailors' because the Chinese perceived their British masters to all have red hair. Today they still use the Imperial system of feet and inches and embrace British techniques in garment-making.

The Hongbang tailors are famous for initiating the 'Five First' movement in the development of modern Chinese garments. They created the Chinese tunic using elements from East and West and this was adopted as the official state suit. They opened the first Chinese Tailor and Outfitter store, offering handcrafted bespoke garments and founded the Hongbang School of Tailoring.

After the revolution in 1949, attitudes towards the West – as well as ideas about fashion, conformity and virtually everything else – underwent huge changes. Most of the tailors who could, left for Hong Kong or Taiwan. Taiwan never achieved the kind of status for tailoring that Shanghai once had. Hong Kong enjoyed a reputation for cheap prices and quality work but the Chinese tailors there have since been largely supplanted by Indian suit-makers. I investigated Ningbo city as a site for my business idea because of its history; many tailors there still use inches and their skills had been handed down from one generation to the next.

My family in Ningbo offered to look for a tailoring workshop or a master tailor whom I could work with, to provide a traditional Savile Row bespoke tailoring service to tailors in the UK. They soon came back with a few names of people and tailoring workshops I could talk to so I flew to China the next day.

On arriving in China, it was suggested by one of my relatives that I should meet the owners of a tailoring workshop in Hangzhou. I took a train from Ningbo to Hangzhou, which took three hours to cover one hundred miles. In those days there was no bullet train to cover the distance in just 46 minutes. I was very impressed when the owners told me that their tailoring brand was well established in mainland China and Hong Kong, with a company history going back over 100 years. The owners took me to visit their tailoring workshop and I was introduced to the master tailor Mr Gu Hong and his wife who were originally from Ningbo. Previously they had worked in Shanghai for over ten years for Kilgour, a well-known tailoring company in Savile Row. In 2004, they began working for this company in Hangzhou.

I told them my plan of offering a bespoke tailoring service to Savile Row and other tailors in the UK, but to do this I would need a sample handmade suit to show the tailors in London the quality of the garments we could produce. All of them agreed to make me a sample suit before I went back to London.

I now had to find a Savile Row company that wanted to work with us. Barry and I wrote letters to all the Savile Row tailors introducing ourselves and outlining our proposal. All, except one, declined to meet us – but we got to meet the oldest tailoring company in Savile Row. I was excited to have someone who wanted to see us but at the same time extremely nervous about meeting with one of the top Savile Row tailoring companies. They liked our proposal because they had a lot of orders but not enough tailors to make them. The owner, Alan Bennett, was also impressed with the quality of our bespoke suit and thought, with a few minor changes, it could be up to the standard they required. I suggested he could go to China with me to train the tailors to Savile Row standard and I was over the moon when Alan agreed. As no one from the workshop in Hangzhou could understand English, I had to learn tailoring craftsmanship, procedure and the terminology so that I could transfer the knowledge to the tailors in China properly. For the next three months, I went to Savile Row to grasp the tailoring knowledge to set up a bilingual order form together so that the tailors in Hangzhou would understand garment requirements from the British tailors.

While I was studying tailoring skills in Savile Row, Alan sent some bespoke garment orders to the workshop in Hangzhou as a test, to see what else needed to be improved. To my relief, he was very satisfied with the quality and speed of their work and the delivery time.

However, he found it very strange that all the metal hooks and bars on the trousers were rusted when they arrived in Savile Row. I told Alan it might be the moisture and temperature difference between China and the UK during transportation and I would check what kinds of packaging could best avoid it. I thoroughly enjoyed my time with the tailors in Savile Row. They also taught me some of the tailoring terms – for example 'whistle and flute' is Cockney rhyming slang for suit, 'doctor' means alteration tailor, 'pig' means an unclaimed garment, 'striker' means a cutter's assistant, 'drummer' means trousers maker, 'crushed beetles' means badly made button holes, 'small seams' is a warning phrase used when someone being discussed is approaching. I love the fact that 'my old China' is well-known Cockney 'double' rhyming slang for a good friend. Apparently, some time ago the best crockery in the UK was called China Plate, which rhymes with mate – hence 'my old China'!

In August 2006, Alan, along with Dennis Cooper, who was a well-respected master tailor in Savile Row, went to Hangzhou with me. It was their first trip to China and they were both very excited.

The owner picked us up from our hotel to take us to the workshop where the temperature was already 38 degrees Celsius outside but even hotter inside with the heat from the irons. Both Alan and Dennis were wearing suits and ties and asked the owners why the air conditioning was not on. The owner told them that there was no air conditioning as he did not think the tailors needed it. So for the next five days, Alan and Dennis gave their training course in a very hot workshop without their jacket and tie and with their shirt sleeves rolled up. All the tailors were also sweating and it was then that Alan realised it was sweat that was causing the metal hooks and bars on the trousers to start rusting.

After completing the training, we decided to visit each tailor in the dormitory attached to the workshop to thank them for their hard work and give them some money. When we met with the master tailor Hong and his wife in their room, she started crying and told us how unhappy they were working there. The owners of the business had promised them that after one year, they would get a 10% share in the company and bonuses, but didn't keep their promise. They were still living in a dormitory attached to the workshop even though the owners had promised to find them a house. They also told us how unhappy they were with their working conditions. In the winter, there was no heating and the tailors had to wear thick coats and mittens to keep warm in temperatures of -2 degrees Celsius. This made it very awkward for the tailors to sew. In summer, there was no air-conditioning and everyone was sweating in temperatures over 40 degrees Celsius. They particularly missed their son and parents back in Ningbo and would prefer to be working there.

Alan and I agreed to talk to the owners about improving the working environment. Unfortunately, the response from them was very dismissive "The tailors are like dogs and they don't need air-conditioning or heating." I was shocked by their totally inhumane attitude! I was also disappointed to discover that the company's 100-year history was also not true. In fact, in 2004 they had registered the brand name in China of a Hong Kong company which had been established for 100 years.

On the flight back, Alan told me he could not work

with the current workshop in Hangzhou but would be willing to support the master tailor Hong in setting up a workshop in Ningbo.

When I got back to the UK, I called the master tailor Hong with the proposal that I would set up a workshop in Ningbo with him in charge. He readily agreed but told me he had to give three months' notice to his employer. I assured him this would be fine as it would give us time to find a new workshop and recruit some good tailors in Ningbo. So four months later, Alan and Dennis went on their second trip to China to train the tailors in the new workshop. After our hard work, the business was up and running. Over the years, some of the top Savile Row tailors have visited our workshop to train our tailors.

Nowadays, many Ningbo-born Hongbang tailors like Hong, work in other cities, and they can only visit their families in Ningbo once a year during the Chinese New Year holiday. But they miss their children and families a lot, which has a detrimental effect on the meticulous craftsmanship required to make high-quality bespoke garments, which are works of art. This was the main reason I set up the workshop in Ningbo. I am also proud of dispelling the stigma that 'Made in China' is a sign of bad quality.

I named the business 'Henry Bailey Limited'. The industry was close to my heart and recalled my roots, helping my mother thread needles as a boy when she was a tailor. I remembered the bright, shining material that danced in the candlelight at Chinese New Year, when she was always fully booked with commissions for new, celebratory bespoke clothes.

I've realised the importance of being in the right place at the right time. Bespoke tailoring in London now has many young apprentices and to set up a business like mine would be difficult today. It has taught me the importance of taking an opportunity when you see it.

In 2008, Henry Bailey Limited was performing well, so I believed it was an opportune time to hire a sales manager to facilitate business growth. This would also free up my time to explore additional business ventures. In June, we brought on board an individual with tailoring experience in London for the role. After training him and introducing him to our client base, I was able to focus on my consultancy business in both China and the UK. This arrangement worked smoothly for several years.

However, intermittent issues did arise, particularly conflicts provoked by the sales manager. These disputes had a negative impact on my working relationship with Barry, who held the position of customer service manager. What compounded the issue was the sales manager suggesting to our clients that, in his opinion, both Barry and I were not putting in enough effort, citing that he was the only one making client visits.

In 2014, I arranged for one of China's largest men's fashion retailers to come to London to discuss a partnership with Henry Bailey Limited. This would bring the quality of a London bespoke tailor to their shops. The partnership was signed in February 2015 for a period of one year, with a possible extension if the project went well.

To my surprise and disappointment, the sales manager we had recruited felt this particular project of Henry in management consultancy for thirty years with many leading companies to help improve their business operation and management. He lived in the same town as me and over the next few months, we became good friends. Following a business trip to China to set up a supply chain consultancy in China, Philip decided to join my business and we have worked together since then.

In 2012, I was invited by the Maltese Prime Minister to attend the 'This Is Malta' event in London for a number of large businesses who had invested in Malta. Another exciting opportunity within the entertainment industry presented itself in 2013. Jeffrey Taylor, a film producer and a friend of many years, invited me to join Stagescreen Productions, based both in London and Los Angeles. China was beginning to play an increasingly important role in the global film industry. It was good to be able to use my experience in the 'real' business world and enter, shall we say, the 'reel' world. It was a different model of working that required an understanding of pop-culture and how the revealed tropes and patterns from China and the UK could work together. Take heroes and heroines, for instance: in China, heroes almost always die at the end of the story whereas the opposite is true in the West. We agreed that younger audiences, wherever they were based, wanted more or less the same thing.

I was struck, initially, by the fact that the film industry was a very different beast to the sorts of businesses I had hitherto been working with. In film-making good and bad behaviour is universal. It was useful to see, too, that having expertise in different fields was not necessarily a benefit when it came to the film and television industries. It took me some time to appreciate how it all functioned, but I always want to learn and add to my areas of expertise. We have a lot of exciting film and television projects in the pipeline and believe we have an international edge that will see success both in China and more widely, around the world.

Life kept moving at a lightning speed. I advised SCALA Consulting Ltd in the UK and Ocean Group in China, on logistics and supply-chain issues. In 2019, I was invited to be a keynote speaker at the China-Britain Trade Expo, the UK's leading China business conference, held at the Queen Elizabeth II Centre in London.

I was aware that I should not have all my eggs in one basket so I have built appropriate teams to run and manage a variety of businesses. My early experiences in the UK have proved invaluable; I am now able to adapt to new places and situations much more readily and to appreciate the differences in culture around the world rather than feeling resistant to them. In 2021, I had the privilege of collaborating with the charity, Young Enterprise, mentoring Master of Business Administration students from the University of Hertfordshire on establishing and managing a business in the UK. A recurring question posed by these budding professionals was, "What defines an entrepreneur?" I often shared my perspective that being an entrepreneur involves managing multiple projects and recognising that having diverse ventures helps protect against the unexpected. It's about using your resources smartly, much like spreading your risks instead of focusing only on one thing. Success is rooted in both good planning and detailed research. What I really think defines an entrepreneur though, is their skill in bringing together a strong, dependable team of specialists, not just employees. Each member brings unique talents that drive the business forward. This teamwork gives entrepreneurs the freedom to always look for new chances.

It is interesting to share here that, as my journey progressed, so did Jenny's. Although I did not meet Jenny until I was 30 years old, we have developed a deep and lasting friendship and she regards me as her brother.

In 2002, Jenny went to work in the USA. Unfortunately, her mother developed lung cancer in 2000 and sadly died in 2005. Her father didn't tell her the seriousness of her mum's cancer so that Jenny could focus on her career in America. Jenny told me that the biggest regret was that she didn't get the chance to visit her mother before she passed away.

Jenny decided to emigrate to Vancouver in 2015 and continues to live in Canada. She has become a very successful entrepreneur there by facilitating trade and investment between North America and China. Jenny gave birth to a baby girl with her partner in March 2020. She is in regular contact with my mum and would like her to visit 'her family' in Vancouver soon. Jenny always calls my mother 'Mum' which shows the great relationship they have. Our mum is also very proud of what Jenny has achieved in her life and career so far and hopes that will continue well into the future.

When I set out to write this chapter, the aim was to share what shaped me and the business opportunities that I took. The content has been carefully chosen to highlight the choices I have had and the teams I created to bring them to life and enable them to continue to prosper.

In the complex web of business and life, "Onwards and Upwards" stands as a testament to the power of seizing opportunities, nurturing relationships and continually adapting. From the bustling workshops of Ningbo to the cinematic canvases of the global film industry, the journey has been both enlightening and challenging. Just as the needles and threads from childhood memories represented a foundation, so too have the experiences detailed in this chapter woven into the sturdy structure of entrepreneurship. Alongside business achievements, the intertwining personal tales, like that of Jenny, highlight the profound impact of connections, both familial and forged. As each page of this chapter has revealed, success is not merely about commercial triumphs but also about the stories we create, the bonds we cherish, and the legacy we leave behind. Here's to always moving onwards and upwards, embracing every challenge and opportunity with gusto and grace.

CHAPTER SEVENTEEN: GEORGE BRUMMELL - THE WORLD'S FIRST DANDY

On a few of my trips to China, a number of my Chinese business contacts, who were aware that I worked with Savile Row tailors, asked if I could arrange to have a British bespoke suit made for each of them, because they admired the Savile Row suit that I wore. In China, most suits are Italian-style with a shorter and more tightly fitting jacket. However, some of the newly affluent were looking to dress differently without compromising quality and craftsmanship. A British-style bespoke suit has a more formal and traditional fit, which appealed to many of the wealthy clients I met. There was a gap in the luxury bespoke tailoring market in China.

After consultation with Barry and Philip, I concluded that

this could be a good opportunity to start my own retail brand to sell British-style bespoke suits to individual customers. My first task was to come up with a name for the company. A few days later, I happened to be walking down Jermyn Street in London and came across a statue inscribed with the words:

Beau Brummell, 1778 – 1840. To be truly elegant one should not be noticed. George 'Beau' Brummell's connections with Court, clubs and tailoring embody the spirit of St James's past and present.

I wondered if there was a company called George Brummell or Beau Brummell?

My research on him came up with the following:

George Brummell, the Englishman of Fashion known as "Beau" Brummell and famous for his friendship with the Prince of Wales (later King George IV), was the undisputed leader of fashion at the beginning of the 19th century. From his early years, George Brummell paid great attention to his dress code. As a result of his friendship with the Prince of Wales and his own good taste in dress, he became an iconic figure of men's fashion in the UK. George Brummell was born in 1778 in Downing Street, London. He created the then fashionable style of men's dress, with perfectly fitted and tailored individually made bespoke garments. This look was based on dark coats, full-length trousers rather than knee breeches and stockings, and, to complete the look, an immaculate linen shirt and elaborately knotted cravat. He is credited with introducing and establishing as fashion the modern men's suit, worn with a necktie. Tailoring has been associated with Savile Row since the for promoting their fabrics in China they supplied us with fabric at a discounted rate. The theme for the event was to be "The evolving story of British bespoke clothing for men". Frank had to design and cut forty different suits to present a history of British Menswear from the early nineteenth century to the present day and into the future.

Making forty bespoke suits for men that we had never met was a big ask as they had to look like a perfect fit on each of the models. Frank suggested we got 20 models, all within an inch or so of each other in height and with similar chest and waist measurements, then he would have a standard size to cut the suits.

Frank worked closely with Guy and Holly from 'Dashing Tweeds' who were supplying some of the fabrics. They grouped the suits into different styles and eras and selected music for each period. At the same time, I was liaising with the festival organiser about our strict measurement requirements for the models and also searching for a sponsor to help cover some of the quickly mounting costs.

Two months before the event I talked to the company selling British-made Aston Martin cars in Ningbo and, when I explained the aim of the show was to highlight British bespoke tailoring culture and luxury men's fashion, they readily agreed to be a sponsor.

Before leaving for China we had to source the various accessories we would need, such as riding boots and jodhpurs to go with the red hunting jacket. The one item we couldn't take with us to China was a double-barrelled shot gun to go with the game keepers' Norfolk jacket. I asked one of my contacts in China if he could find one for us and, to our delight, he found us a triple-barrelled shotgun which looked stunning and, to everyone's surprise, was a cigarette lighter!

The other thing I learnt about fashion shows is the limited amount of time you get with the fashion models. At first, we were told they would only be available in the afternoon before the event. Having explained that each of the 20 models would need to be fitted into two bespoke suits and alterations made to ensure the fit looked perfect it was arranged that we could meet them two nights before the event. That was a long night for everyone with Frank selecting which model would look best in each outfit, and some of my workshop tailors making last minute alterations to ensure the perfect fit.

At the rehearsal, one of the models came on stage with his shirt undone and his bow tie crooked. Because we were bringing the models on in groups, the turnaround time for some of them was quite short and this model only had 4 minutes 35 seconds to get out of his first suit and put on a dress shirt with studs, dinner jacket, trousers, shoes and a bow tie. We had two well-trained dressers to help each model but this particular one would need more help so we had four dressers waiting for him for his costume change. On stage, the models were the epitome of relaxed elegance but out back it was like a Formula 1 pit stop with each model rushing to their assigned changing area, stripping down, being re-dressed then inspected before going back on stage. Did it go well on the night? Yes – it was a great success. There were eight hundred people in the audience which included many from the men's fashion industry; 28 media companies and the owners of China's two largest menswear companies. It was shown on two TV channels. The media coverage we received was highly positive.

The next three days were spent on a stand at the exhibition. Frank demonstrated how to cut patterns with the help of another master tailor, Andrew Livingston. He had been sent to look at our tailoring workshop by one of the top London tailors but had volunteered to help us with the show and the exhibition. In the evening, after being on the stand, Frank was having to measure and fit clients in his hotel room and by the end of the exhibition, he had remembered why he had wanted to retire! He told me that he would be returning to the UK and back into retirement. I took the opportunity to speak with Andrew Livingston and he told me that, although he worked for Savile Row tailors, he wasn't employed by them as he had his own business in Scotland so would be very interested in working with me in China.

After the catwalk show, I received an invitation to give a smaller show in Nantong, in Jiangsu province, at an event being organised by the owner of a large clothing manufacturer. It was in two days' time and neither Philip nor I were tailors but, with some trepidation, we decided to do it.

This proved to be a wise decision as the owner of the company wanted to offer his clients Savile Row quality bespoke suits in his new shop in Nantong. We agreed we could visit every three months to measure and fit his clients. The marketing and catwalk shows had worked, and we had reached the point where we were now a new brand name that people wanted to work with. I offered Andrew the role of Head Cutter for George Brummell Ltd. In the intricate world of tailoring, the Head Cutter is more than a skilled hand with scissors. Andrew would serve as an artisan responsible for drafting initial patterns, advising on design, and overseeing the entire tailoring process. He became our quality linchpin, ensuring each stitch honoured the distinguished traditions of Savile Row craftsmanship. Andrew is the fourth generation of his family to be a master tailor and he has worked with many high profile clients, including members of the Royal family.

Andrew, like Frank, is a perfectionist when it comes to making suits, but he had to get used to working in less than perfect environments. Many clients do not have time to come to be measured and expect the tailor to visit them. So besides visiting the shop in Nantong we also had to go to other cities including Shanghai, Suzhou, Beijing, Shijiazhuang Zhengzhou, Dalian and Hangzhou. Once we were asked to measure a police chief for a suit but had to be at his office within the hour. As our driver raced to get there we wondered, if we were stopped for speeding, would he tell the police officers that we were on the way to see their boss. When we got to the police building, we were ushered into a storeroom with lots of boxes and a nine foot tall statue of an elephant. The police chief told us he had a meeting and did not want to keep us waiting and this was the only empty room available – apart from the elephant of course.

Another time we were in Shanghai and had been asked to measure a leading chef at an exclusive private club. He could only see us after he had finished preparing the evening meals so it was about 11:00pm when he took us out onto his rooftop terrace overlooking the river and the bright lights of Shanghai. The view was amazing but

Andrew kept mumbling under his breath how difficult it was to measure someone in the dark especially when they were wearing a black Bruce Lee outfit.

Andrew's wife, Sue, who managed their clothes shop in Scotland, came to China with Andrew on one trip and I found her to be an excellent salesperson. She would show the clients the different fabrics and when they were not sure which to choose she would suggest they have two suits made which they often did. After that Sue became a permanent member of our team. Andrew would measure the clients, cut the suits and make them back in Scotland. Sue would be in charge of the fabrics and explain the differences between them whilst educating clients in British dressing etiquette. Philip was responsible for the company accounts but would assist Andrew with measurements. He also learnt more of the Chinese language. My role was to use my network in China to seek wealthy clients, translate and make all the travel arrangements. We all got on well as a team and became very good friends. Although the trips involved long working days we managed to have a lot of happy times. When I introduced everyone to clients, I would start off by saying "Andrew is Scottish, Sue is English, Philip is Welsh, but I am a real British person."

We were all going to places we had never been to before so I got to experience local traditions and a vast variety of food. On one occasion we were invited to dinner by the general manager of a large men's clothing retailer and the meal started with what looked like dumpling soup. I noticed that our host wasn't eating his so neither did I and asked him in Chinese about the soup. Andrew and Philip were busy eating their dumplings when they noticed I hadn't started mine. Andrew asked,

"Biao, why haven't you eaten your dumplings? They are delicious"

"Because it's not a dumpling. It's a chopped-up donkey's penis!", I replied.

The look on both their faces of shock and horror was very amusing and it was difficult to not laugh out loud.

A bespoke suit is made to fit the one person it has been designed for so cannot be sold to someone else. I explained to potential clients that we needed to order and pay for the fabric and trimmings before we made them a bespoke suit so needed to be paid in advance. They accepted this, so we never had any problems with bad debts. A lady in Beijing came to select the fabric for her husband who was due to see us the next day to be measured. His flight to Beijing was cancelled but she had already transferred the money to me so I said I would return it but she insisted that we keep it for the waste of our time. I couldn't accept this but when she said she had a son working in London we agreed to make him a suit when we got back to the UK. This we did and he was very pleased with his bespoke suit.

We were getting more orders in Beijing than any other city and were looking for a base there to store and display our fabrics and some sample suits. I was introduced to Lisa who had an office and a traditional courtyard with rooms in Prince Gong Palace. She was very keen to work with us and offered us the use of two rooms in the Palace to meet our clients. I must admit when I showed the address to prospective clients they were intrigued to know that part of the palace that was closed to the public was reserved for us.

One of our partners in China had a cashmere business and wanted us to make suits for some of his important clients using his own cashmere cloth. It was interesting to visit his factory in Hebei province where he had his own goat farms. His factory took the wool and turned it into different cashmere yarns used for producing cashmere jumpers and suit fabrics. He also had his own retail shops. We received a lot of suit orders from him and every time we visited he arranged for us to have a cashmere goat barbecue. Although it tasted good, I always felt upset that one of the baby goats had been killed for us to eat. After our fourth visit, I asked him politely if he could refrain from the slaughter of one of his goats to which he readily agreed.

Some of our Chinese clients like to have fittings when they are visiting the UK. On one occasion a client flew to Edinburgh just to be measured for a suit by Andrew but when Andrew got to the hotel he realised the client did not speak any English. I had to translate their conversation over the phone. One advantage of clients visiting Andrew is that I got the opportunity to visit Scotland. I do like Edinburgh with its mix of wide, open streets in the Georgian New Town and the narrow passages of the Medieval Old Town. The city is steeped in history and Scottish heritage and traditions. The visits of so many Chinese to Andrew's workshop in Castle Douglas attracted the attention of the Dumfries and Galloway Life magazine which gave him an award for excellence in exports in 2019.

The success of George Brummell was advantageous in

more ways than one. Most of its clients are high net worth individuals. I would talk to them not just about having a bespoke suit made but also about the investment opportunities in the UK which I could help them with through Buckingham Wealth.

As I reflect on the extraordinary journey that brought us from Savile Row's hallowed workshops to bustling cities across China, I can't help but marvel at how far George Brummell Ltd has come. We've stitched together not just suits, but relationships – bridging cultural gaps with threads of trust and fabric swatches. We've tailored a brand that transcends borders, elevated by the expertise of masters like Andrew and the invaluable support of Sue and Philip. And yet, as we measure up our success, the tape is still unspooling, stretching towards new opportunities and challenges that await us. 'Carpe Diem' has been our motto, and as we prepare for our next chapter – perhaps in yet unexplored markets or unexpected collaborations – the sentiment rings truer than ever: Seize the Day.

CHAPTER EIGHTEEN: LEARNING CURVES

If you'd told me years ago that so much of my professional career would revolve around public speaking, I wouldn't have believed you. My presentation titles have included: *Gain the Competitive Edge with Knowledge on Chinese Business Culture; Chinese Business Culture: The Essential Rule in China; Know the Game; China's Emergence: An Awakened Dragon* and *How to Cooperate with China in the Fashion Industry*. These titles, meant to give a flavour of my discussions, have been well-received and well-attended from Moscow to Malta and I hope have contributed to the sum of understanding about the land I once called home.

As I learnt more about the process of public speaking generally, I also began to understand more of other cultures and how they responded to these talks. I was now both a British citizen and a Chinese one and it was apparent that there were vast differences between not only these two nations but so many others, too. For example, in Moscow, I was due to talk to the MBA students about the impact of the cultural differences between China and Russia on the negotiation process so that the students could develop their negotiation skills appropriately. I've always looked quite young in appearance and a friend suggested this might be a problem. In Russia, as in China respect for those older than oneself is extremely important.

"Look," said my friend, "I know a barbershop where they can cut your hair and make it into a moustache for you. That'll make you look old and wise!"

I was very keen to look the part in front of the students at Moscow State University, so I followed this advice and was soon walking through the lecture theatre with my brand-new moustache. Of course, Russia is one of the coldest places on earth and that day it was –12 degrees Celsius. The heating, therefore, was cranked up about as high as it would go and I was wearing a thick suit and a tie. I began to sweat and within moments – just as I'd started my talk – the moustache began to peel off! Thankfully, everyone laughed. I explained the reason I'd done it which made people more sympathetic to me and reinforced that you shouldn't judge a book by its cover.

I received the following recommendation letter after my visit:

Lomonosov Moscow State University's Institute of Asian and African Studies and the Centre for Intercultural Communication L.L.C. had the honour of receiving Professor Biao Wang, Founder and CEO of Camellia Universal Limited, in Moscow on 8 and 9 April 2011 as a visiting lecturer on Doing Business in China. During three months of our collaboration, Professor Wang proved a person of high integrity and professionalism. Before coming to Moscow to deliver his lectures, Professor Wang was the most active contributor to the curriculum design process, promptly responding to all messages and comments, suggesting new ideas and offering expertise on China-related topics. His lectures were of such a great value that he was the only visiting lecturer who received an official commendation for the enormous contribution he made to the program. I recommend Professor Wang without any hesitation as an experienced China business consultant and a talented public speaker. Fedor Ovchinnikov, Lomonosov Moscow State University's Institute of Asian and African Studies and the Centre for Intercultural Communication L.L.C, Director, Russia.

Needless to say, I was terribly flattered by their response but decided not to put 'professor' on my business card!

I'd had thought that Russia which is, in many ways, more restrictive in its laws and customs than many other countries would be a tough place to visit. The UK, in comparison, is so liberal and progressive in its way of thinking and its expectations of its citizens. I was surprised to find how much I enjoyed visiting Moscow and seeing all the sights – especially Red Square. The people I met were very friendly which was not what I was expecting from the news reports I had heard over the years about Russia.

Often, I'd arrive to give these talks and be mistaken for a student or one of the translators. Once, on live TV in China, Philip was asked to speak and I was translating.

"We don't need a translator in the picture," the director told the cameraman. Fortunately, one of my assistants was there to explain, "Actually, he's the business owner…"

and I was hastily put back into the picture.

This might sound infuriating but it can work to my advantage. When we met a potential business partner in China, I would introduce myself as the company's representative there. I knew that if a CEO later contacted my British colleagues directly, without going through me, they were not trustworthy, because they wanted to cut me out to save on my commission. As a result, they wouldn't be considered as long-term partners and it proved to be a good litmus test for future partnerships. It's so important to show respect for everyone, whoever they are and whatever they do.

Over the years, experience has taught me a great deal – from the tentative start at public speaking to mastering the art of real engagement between myself and different audiences. The latter can only come after careful research and understanding to be able to confidently deliver the topic. On reflection, I have had a tendency to 'dream big' since childhood. The bigger picture starts with working on an idea in isolation. If it stands up to scrutiny then I share it with my team so that it can be tested and developed further. In the diverse global world of business, I soon learnt that it was important to be able to work from anywhere. Fortunately, in the digital world of today, the power of the internet and social media for business purposes enables constant contact across all time zones. My genuine interest in people has led to good, strong relationships with clients and is a key driver in the retention and development of any profitable business partnership. I have learned that it is vital to embrace change and support clients through it to the benefit of their business and mine. 'Smart working' – the use of time to its best advantage – is something I have taken on board and try to adopt in everything I do in my work.

Education, hard work and determination have enabled me to make the most of my life so far. As a result, I always encourage others, especially young people, to take advantage of their education.

Not all business opportunities are easy and straightforward but not giving up and seeing them through has made me a much stronger person.

I have seen people who think it is all too easy to sit back and wait for things to happen – that wait could, however, be a lifetime. You have to be proactive and make things happen. This has been an essential element in the transformation of my life.

With all this work and travel, and the mental energy it requires, there needs to be a release mechanism of some sort. It had become obvious that if I was to maintain a balance in my life, I needed something totally different from my work life. Around May 2008, Bryon encouraged me to play table tennis again. I now play a few times a week in different leagues and find it deeply relaxing. I've made a lot of good friends, such as Howard Craig, Marc Lyons, Jez Wilcox, and Bernie Raffe, a professional photographer, who often picks me up to go to different venues. Table tennis even enables me to come up with better business ideas. I have a machine at home, so I can play whenever I like. In 2023, I had the honour of receiving 'The Presidents Trophy' from the Milton Keynes Table Tennis League, an award given to an individual who has notably impacted the sport. While my name may be on the trophy, the real credit goes to a collaborative effort.

Bernie Raffe has been instrumental in this journey. Both of us have poured our time and energy into revitalising the Leighton Buzzard Table Tennis Club. We've not only attracted new players to join our ranks but also secured a fresh venue for our activities. Additionally, we debuted a new logo, thoughtfully crafted by Richard Clarke, which has helped to garner more attention for the club. Thus, this award is not a solo achievement; it's a reflection of the united spirit and contributions of everyone involved.

I've learned a lot from people around me, and I try to give back when I can. I picked up some computer skills on my own and have been able to help friends who find tech confusing. Not long after moving to the UK, I had the chance to teach some basic computer skills to older people. My mum and grandparents always showed me that it's good to help others, so I'm just following their example. I'm glad when I can sort out a problem or make something easier for someone. Beyond that, I care deeply about community issues. My fundraising and advocacy work have had a positive impact on Leighton Linslade Homeless Service, Luton & Dunstable Hospital, and the Sue Ryder charity. It just goes to show what kindness and community involvement can achieve.

One winter, I got a call from Mrs. Williams, one of the older ladies from the computer class. She was quite upset because her computer wouldn't start, and it held all her family photos. I went over to her place and found that the power cable was just unplugged. Plugging it back in fixed the problem and she was really relieved.

She thanked me and said, "You didn't just fix my computer; you gave me back my family photos." That made me realise that even small things can mean a lot to someone else. It also reminded me why it's good to be involved in your community, whether that's helping someone with their computer or doing some fundraising.

During my time working with the University of Hertfordshire, my role was to guide aspiring MBA students in the intricacies of establishing, operating, and managing a business within the UK context. I covered various aspects of business management, from formulating a business plan to understanding market dynamics and implementing effective leadership strategies.

Yet, this experience wasn't just a one-way street; it was a mutually enriching journey. While I may have been the mentor in the formal sense, the students offered me a fresh perspective on various aspects of business. Their innovative ideas, enthusiasm, and questions prompted me to reflect on my own practices and consider new approaches to problem-solving. It was an enlightening experience that underscored the value of continuous learning in professional life. Thus, even as I provided guidance, I also gained valuable insights that have enriched my own understanding of the business landscape.

Travel is very refreshing. Visiting new places opens your eyes, pushes you out of your comfort zone and expands your horizons. I aim to arrange more holidays in the future. There is nothing quite like the heady mixture of nervousness, trepidation and excitement when one first touches down in a place one has never been before. It shocks the brain into action, into activity, and energises the soul. As to the scope of travel and mode of transport, the UK is much smaller than China and train travel is somewhat slower! Nevertheless, I've found some places with amazing scenic views which have reminded me of the mountains of my childhood. I am enjoying the journey of embracing both cultures. Taking time to enjoy what is around me is now part of my life and I thoroughly recommend it.

To keep pace and stay ahead of the game I follow the news feeds on social media, using, especially, Google News, BBC News, BBC Alerts, The Financial Times and the China News App on a daily basis. Within the fashion/bespoke tailoring business, Andrew and I share news regularly on trends and styles. To keep in touch with business colleagues in China, I have set up a workgroup on the messaging app 'WeChat'. It is important to solve issues without delays caused by the time difference between the two countries which can/could affect deadlines.

I find music relaxing and soothing. If I feel down, I listen to Whitney Houston. If I need motivation, I have Luciano Pavarotti and if I feel happy there's always Michael Jackson.

I also take great pleasure in the people I'm lucky enough to call my friends. I have a diverse mix of people from backgrounds similar to mine and those whose beginnings could not be more different. One of those is Roger, who had been the CEO of a UK charity. He also became a good friend of Bryon's and would visit him twice a week and take him out for lunch to various places. I also value the time spent conversing on a wide range of topics with friends over a meal. It might sound strange, but it still feels like a luxury to me to go out for coffee with people just for a chat. I can talk to Lisa or Patricia about everything and anything. James comes to my rescue with DIY. I am making up for the lost time in China when I had little time to potter, wander or meet casually with friends for a drink due to the demands of my studies. Now I religiously make time to do all three. It's important to me that friendships are nurtured.

I have to admit that television is one of my escapes. I watch scary films, anything sci-fi is a must, plus educational programmes about countries and their cultures around the world. Space and the universe fascinate me. I believe there are other life forms beyond our earth. I can also boast (well share at least) that I have collected 128 sets of coins from different countries which tell me a lot about their histories and cultures. I have not visited that many countries – well not yet!

One of the best ways to relieve stress is through gardening. I love exploring nature through the planting and cultivating of flowers, shrubs and trees. I enjoy observing the fruits of hard work in the transformation of a thriving plant. It doesn't escape me, either, that gardening is a very British pastime – adopted readily into my own daily life. I seem to have green fingers from the evidence of my back garden. There are thriving pear, apple, cherry and plum trees. Rhubarb seems to flourish and I have been successful with tomato plants and a few herbs. A watermelon is growing really well in my conservatory at the time of writing. Some of this may be down to luck, but I like to think I'm reconnecting with the farming skills I learnt from my parents all those years ago in my birth village.

I have a deep affection for Bedfordshire, so it was a natural choice for me to move to Leighton Buzzard, one of its historic market towns, back in 2012. The town offers a quiet and peaceful atmosphere, not to mention its proximity to Whipsnade Zoo. My local area is graced with Astral Lake Park, which had become my go-to spot for exercise during the ongoing coronavirus restrictions. The park offers scenic walkways, including a route along a section of the Grand Union Canal, which stretches all the way from Birmingham to London. Though I haven't ventured that far, the walks have introduced me to a diverse range of wildlife. On one occasion, I even had to navigate around a heron that seemed entirely unfazed by my presence.

It feels particularly nice to be able to invite my mum, dad and sister to come and visit me – and have the space to accommodate them comfortably. They come over every year or so. My sister works so hard on her steel business and doesn't have much free time between work and family life. But when they do come, they stay for a good long time and we enjoy many sightseeing activities while relaxing together.

In summary, the journey of life, for me, has been a fascinating blend of learning curves and rich experiences. Whether it's dealing with the challenges of public speaking across cultures, nurturing diverse friendships, or finding solace in table tennis and community service, each chapter has enriched me in some way. It's not just about the destination but the ride along the way – the hardships, the triumphs, and the invaluable lessons. Even the setbacks have been stepping stones, helping me to gain a deeper understanding of myself and the world around me.

So, if there's one thing I'd like everyone to take away from my story so far, it's this: never stop learning, because life never stops teaching.

CHAPTER NINETEEN: MY SISTER - THE 'IRON QUEEN'

My sister Tiejun has been the unsung hero in the story of my life. When we talk, she fills the air with praise for my accomplishments, eagerly sharing my story with anyone who will listen. It might have been easy for her to harbour feelings of jealousy, especially given the educational paths that were open to me and not to her. Yet, not once has she made me feel a shred of guilt.

When we were growing up, she was more than just a sister; she was almost a second mum to me. Her sacrifices began early, making tough choices that would shape both of our futures. As she tirelessly worked to turn both her dreams and mine into realities, her influence became the bedrock upon which my life was built. This chapter aims to honour her, to ensure that her incredible story is not lost in the shadow of my own.

My sister was born in 1972 and her name, Tiejun Fan, means 'Iron Queen'. Our parents were busy working in order to put the food on the table so it fell to our father's mother to look after my sister. She developed a very close relationship with our paternal grandmother and wishes she was still with us to see and enjoy the transformation in our family situation.

Quite often I dream about the fun of our childhood: climbing mountains together; taking our family ox to green fields; catching fish in rivers and loaches in ditches. When Tiejun was about 13 years old and I was seven she saw a wallet on the lane not far from our home. She opened it to see if she could find out who owned it so she could return it. However, apart from some money she could not find any ID. So she came up with the idea of going to the village broadcasting studio with me which was around a 25-minute walk from home. Following the lost and found announcement, the owner came forward to collect the wallet. In order to thank my sister, he gave her an orange as a reward. I remembered the orange had a tough shiny skin. Tiejun was reluctant to eat the orange by herself so when she got home she carefully took out each orange segment and shared them with me. It was a real treat as we only ever had oranges at Chinese New Year.

In the 1980s, people in the UK had TV, radio and newspapers for the news. In our village, the only way for public communications was a lot of speakers blaring out the 'news of the day'. It was extremely loud if you were under a loudspeaker so I always put my hands over my ears or kept away from them. However, our paternal grandmother always enjoyed listening to the radio series about farming (a bit like the Archers on BBC Radio Four in the UK).

There were 12 speakers mounted on top of tall and strong wooden posts distributed around the village. The studio would broadcast daily the farming weather forecast, play music and also give the time and date of village meetings and other important messages.

As a small aside, when I later moved to Leighton Buzzard, I couldn't help but fantasise about introducing this sound system. Imagine it: 'Good morning, Leighton Buzzard! Today's bin collection will be delayed by four hours, and don't forget the school fair this Saturday!' I quickly realised, though, that the only noise people want blaring through the streets here is the sweet sound of silence. I suspect if the council ever tried that, they'd have an uprising led by pensioners in slippers and youngsters in noise-cancelling headphones!

In 1989, a year that would change everything for our family, Tiejun found herself at a crossroads. Our parents had just divorced, and the atmosphere at home was heavy with tension and uncertainty. On a particularly chilly evening, Mr Zhang, the head teacher of her school, made an unexpected visit. He looked earnest, his eyes filled with a mix of concern and hope as he sat in our cramped living room.

"Tiejun's academic performance is excellent," Mr Zhang began, his voice tinged with gravity. "She's one of the best students we have. It would truly be a loss for her not to continue her studies in high school. She has a bright future ahead."

My mum turned her gaze to Tiejun, her eyes clouded with a cocktail of emotions – pride, sorrow, and the burden of a heartbreaking decision. "The choice is yours, Tiejun," she said softly.

Tiejun took a moment, her face a canvas of deep contemplation. Then, with a sigh that seemed to carry the weight of the world, she spoke. "I can't go on to high school. I need to work."

What followed for Tiejun was a plunge into the unknown. She'd heard whispers about the rising demand for automotive service technicians, a field dominated by men. Undeterred and fired up with her innate determination, Tiejun decided to seize the opportunity. She became an apprentice at an automobile repair garage in Qiuai, Ningbo.

When she walked in on her first day, the surprise on the faces of the 15 male employees was almost comical. Muffled chuckles and snide comments filled the air, but Tiejun stood her ground. The men soon learned she was no pushover; she refused to be bullied or belittled.

One day she announced she was going to cut her hair short. Apparently, every time she had to slide under a vehicle her fabulous long hair acted like a broom and, by the end of the day, the smell was not good. The following day she got her hair cut really short but it didn't take long to get used to the new style. Tiejun was a quick learner and after a year she passed the exams to become a fully qualified mechanic to train the new apprentices. She showed everyone that a woman can be as good a mechanic as a man, which was groundbreaking at that time. After that, everyone in the company respected her and some of them became lifelong good friends.

Later, I would join in the fun. Almost every day, during my summer holidays I would go to work with my sister and see how the mechanics took a whole car apart and then reassembled it. I would help her clean the car engines and grease the different parts – which was a very dirty job – as it was done by hand. Mum's idea was that one day I might become a mechanic – how far away from the truth was that going to be!

My sister was often on evening duty calls. When a client's car broke down she and her colleagues would be called out to repair it. One winter at midnight she got a call that there was a car broken down on the motorway. It was snowing with a temperature of –7 degrees Celsius. This sounded so exciting that I decided to go with her. When we got there, the driver was freezing as he could not start the car's engine to get heat. My sister quickly gave him her own coat and asked him to sit in their car to keep warm while they were checking his car. It took my sister and her colleagues almost two hours to solve the problem and we got back home at around 4:30am. After sleeping for a couple of hours, Tiejun then went to work at the garage as usual – that is what you call dedication to the job.

In 2018, I took some British clients and colleagues to Ningbo on business. Tiejun was driving and a light started flashing on the dashboard. Tiejun said, "Don't worry, I'll go and check it out". 15 minutes later we were on our way again. My British clients and colleagues looked at each other in surprise and were very impressed with her mechanical skills. I was equally impressed as I am useless when it comes to anything mechanical!

After working at the automobile repair garage for six

years, Tiejun was headhunted, in 1995, by Yinzhou MOT & Road Tax Administration Bureau to use her expertise to help them set up an MOT testing facility and manage a team of six people.

In 1996, she met a medical doctor, Yue Chunlei, through a friend of a friend and they married in the following year. Dr. Yue is four years older than my sister and he is from Chengdu in Sichuan province – renowned for its giant pandas. He moved over one thousand miles to Ningbo to work for Zhejiang Wanli University as a medical clinic doctor and teacher. The university has over 20,000 students. My brother-in-law told me the reason he wanted to move to Ningbo was because he'd read that it was one of the first coastal cities to open to overseas investment and he thought there would be more work opportunities for him there.

Even though our mother had remarried in 1993, four years later she still had not moved in with our stepfather in Hangzhou although they saw each other almost every weekend. For the sake of our mum's happiness, Tiejun and I suggested that she should move to Hangzhou to live with him permanently.

"It is really not fair for both of you to travel over four hours to visit each other every weekend." Tiejun told our mother.

"But what will happen to both of you if I move to Hangzhou," she replied.

"I am married now, Mum. My husband and I will take care of Biao," my sister said. This was a demonstration of the amazing caring attitude which she still displays.

"Don't worry about me, and I will be fine, I am no longer at home anyway, because I am away in boarding school. Besides, you can visit us at any time," I added.

Our mother decided to move to Hangzhou to live with her husband Weimin, his daughter and son. For the next 18 months, Tiejun visited me at school every weekend to check how I was getting on. She'd arrive with all the favourite foods that I couldn't get at the school shop: spicy beef jerky, dried squid, roasted chicken feet, duck's tongue and rice cake. To some Westerners, these foods sound disgusting – but they are great delicacies in China and taste delicious.

In 1999, my sister gave birth to their beautiful son, Yue Tengchao, which means 'super gallop' in Chinese. She and her husband decided to employ a local nanny to help care for him and mum helped from time to time. Two months after giving birth my sister returned to work. She felt now, more than ever, that she must work harder to create better opportunities than she'd had, for her son.

In 2001, our mum's two younger brothers set up Yinzhou New Era Steel Trade Centre with five other investors. Both uncles approached my sister to ask if she could work for them to market and promote the Centre. Her job was to find steel traders who would relocate their offices and warehousing there. My sister felt that the MOT testing facility no longer needed her expertise and relished the challenge of being a sales and marketing manager.

Tiejun is a natural networker and enjoyed meeting and talking with a lot of people from all over China. By the end of her first year, she had managed to sell all four hundred spaces at the Centre. For the next three years, she was responsible for ensuring that the traders were happy with the service she provided.

After working there for four years, Tiejun felt confident that she knew enough about the steel business to be able to set up her own company. Although she was taking a risk, her previous employer told her if things didn't work out she could always go back to work for them. So she borrowed some money from relatives to rent warehouse space and buy steel stocks.

Tiejun had researched the steel market carefully and bought the types of steel that were not supplied by many other companies in Ningbo. She made her first sale within a week of setting up the business.

Using the network of contacts Tiejun had built up in her previous position she quickly expanded her customer base. She sold different types of steel – flat, tubular, angled, channelled, plated stainless, aluminium, galvanised zinc coil plate with a zinc coating, and other custom-made steel products.

In her first year of business, my sister, Tiejun, had to promote, market and sell the steel products as well as keeping the company accounts all by herself. I'll never forget that gloomy winter evening in the UK when my phone buzzed with a call from China. When I picked up, I could immediately sense the tremor in Tiejun's voice, as if she was on the verge of breaking down. "I don't know what to do," she choked out between sobs. "Some clients are really unhappy with the steel quality. They want to return it."

The weight of her words hung heavy in the air. I could

hear the fatigue and desperation in her voice, a far cry from the confident entrepreneur she usually was. "What happens now?" I asked cautiously.

"If they return it, I'm going to lose a lot of money, and it's going to be so difficult to keep the business going," she said, her voice tinged with despair.

After a deep, collective breath, we both agreed that she needed to address this head-on. "You should talk to the clients directly," I advised. "Maybe you can find a way to make it right."

Determined, Tiejun took a series of gruelling bus journeys to visit each disgruntled customer. She walked into those meetings with a mixture of dread and hope, pledging better quality steel for future orders and a 15% discount as a goodwill gesture. When she called me to say that they had all agreed to her proposal, she sounded genuinely relieved but also transformed. The experience had clearly changed her.

"It taught me something invaluable," she reflected later, a new seriousness colouring her words. "People don't just want cheap stuff; they want quality, and they want it at a reasonable price. I've got to focus on learning the nuances of steel quality and where to source the best materials."

When Tiejun started her business, she did not own a car and so it could take her an entire day to visit a single customer. This meant a long journey from Hangzhou to Ningbo for our mum to go into the office to answer the phone and look after the stock. However, after a year Tiejun was able to buy a car which made it much easier for her to visit clients. The company was doing so well that she was also able to pay back the loans she had taken out to start the business.

Every week, like clockwork, my sister and I ring each other to trade stories of triumphs and tribulations in our respective businesses. But our conversations aren't just about work; they're also a lifeline of love and family support. In 2017, a shadow was cast over our lives when our biological father began struggling with his health. His breaths became laboured, each inhale and exhale a whisper of vulnerability. Recognising the gravity of his condition, Tiejun didn't hesitate to open her home and heart. She asked him to come live with her family, so she could be his caregiver, and he gratefully accepted her offer.

Tragically, in October 2020, our father was hospitalised with severe heart and lung complications. In those quiet, sterile corridors where life often hangs in the balance, my father took his last breath. It was the 23rd of October, a day etched into our memories. He passed away peacefully, enveloped in the love of his family, with Tiejun and our mother by his bedside, holding his hands as he ventured into the unknown.

Since starting her business in 2005, Tiejun has worked seven days a week. She has built a reputation as one of the best steel providers in the area and is working with some big listed companies. Many new customers come by word of mouth. My sister told me that this reputation is the result of three things: quality of steel, quality of staff and speed of response. Customer satisfaction is really important to her business and she and her team always aim to provide customers with the best quality at affordable prices. She has built a vast network of loyal clients. Many customers and competitors call her a true 'Iron Queen' which says a lot about her character.

To my surprise, Tiejun has a fascinating relationship with her competitors – they're not just rivals – they're friends. I remember one evening in Ningbo vividly. My British colleagues and I were taken out by one of her 'rival-friends' for an authentic Chinese meal. The atmosphere was electric, filled with laughter and discussions about the steel business. The food was fantastic, and afterwards, we were treated to relaxing foot massages.

"What's the secret?" I couldn't help but ask my sister later. "How have you managed to turn competitors into friends?"

Tiejun looked thoughtful for a moment before responding. "In this industry, it's easy to view everyone as a threat. But I've always found it's more beneficial to build bridges rather than burn them," she said, her eyes gleaming with conviction.

She went on to explain that these friendships have created a network of contacts she can call upon at any time to discuss steel business and various issues affecting them. "When you're up against the same challenges, there's a mutual understanding that's really comforting," she elaborated. "Plus, sometimes a large order comes in and you need to pool resources. Having a competitor you can rely on is a lifesaver in those situations."

When I am in Ningbo on business, she will always help me, like she did when we were children. She told me that her dream was for the whole family to be happy and healthy. She would like to retire early and do some public welfare work like sponsoring educational activities for children who cannot afford school in the poorer mountain areas of China. She would also like to take our mother and stepfather to travel around the world. In many ways, I think my sister takes after our mother in her determination to get things done but also in her desire to help others less fortunate.

Although my sister didn't complete her formal education, she developed her skills to become an extremely well-respected and successful business woman in male dominated industries.

Not a day goes by without me realising how fortunate I am to have a sister like Tiejun Fan. She is an inspiration to me because of everything she did and the sacrifices she made for me in the most amazingly unselfish manner.

As I look back on our lives, filled with trials, joys, and endless lessons, one thread shines unmistakably bright: Tiejun, my Iron Queen. She's more than just a sister; she's a beacon of resilience and a pillar of strength. Her choices were never easy, yet she faced them with a grace and courage that most would find unimaginable. From quitting school at 17 to make family ends meet, to standing her ground in her professional life, she's faced each obstacle like a warrior queen clad in invisible armour.

Yet, what truly marks her as an 'Iron Queen' is not just her ability to withstand the fires of life but to emerge from them even stronger. She has an uncanny knack for turning challenges into stepping stones, making her not just an inspiration to me, but to everyone who knows her. Tiejun's journey hasn't been without its cracks and dents, but just like iron, she has endured, proving that real strength isn't about never breaking; it's about forging ahead, no matter the heat.

In the grand story of our family, she has not just been a character but a potent force, shaping the narrative in ways that will be told and retold for generations. She is, and forever will be, my Iron Queen."

CHAPTER TWENTY: LOOKING AHEAD - NOW AND THE FUTURE

I think about my early life and those carefree days on the mountains. I remember the shouts and laughter of my friends as we played together. All those hours spent cycling, swimming, fishing, climbing trees and watching the animals who had made our mountains their home or maybe it was the other way around? I could never have imagined that my life would progress and evolve in the way it did. It seems unimaginable that a small boy from a quiet village, with barely enough money to attend the local school, would go on to have the sorts of experiences I've been fortunate enough to have.

For me, the importance of curiosity cannot be underestimated. I think of myself as a child and the struggles I faced at school all the while nurturing a hope of learning English. That I might one day become bilingual would have been unlikely, too, but I was certainly determined to try. My own journey has taught me that, even if money is scarce, education can still be pursued. It takes hard work and determination – much harder work than if someone has endless resources at their disposal – but it is certainly possible and definitely worth it. Learning English to the level I achieved was the path to success and to international travel. Without it, I may never have progressed further than my high school or, at the very most, university.

Returning to Wuxiang High School was a delight; I felt I'd come full circle and could see how keen the teachers were to use my story as an example. I had not been especially gifted academically and had never been one for whom top marks came naturally. Indeed, I was always quite average. But with tenacity and determination doors were opened to me. I could have given up at many different stages: when my parents separated, when I moved to live with my maternal grandparents, when my mother remarried and moved or when I was sent to boarding school. None of these events were terrible situations in themselves but each disruption had a massive impact on me. It would have been easy to give up and not try any more: not do the homework, the morning exercises, the eye exercises, the endless hours in the library.

And at university, too, I could have decided enough was enough. It didn't seem fair that some people came from such wealth and privilege to employ private tutors to help them with their studies. If it was like this in academia, what must the real world be like? I could have decided to focus on something besides English or mixed only with Chinese students or abandoned all plans to go abroad. But if I'd done this – any of it – I would only have been hurting myself. It didn't matter to anybody else whether I learned

English and went to the UK or applied for professional, office-based jobs in China and lived with my mother and stepfather. We are only given one life and it's up to us to decide what we do with it.

Money can be both a curse and a blessing as can be evidenced starkly in my own family history with the premature death of my brother in 1976. "He might have survived," my mother told me, sadly, years later, "if we'd had the money to put him in an incubator." It's a strange thing, isn't it? The idea that, if my brother had lived, I may well not have come into the world. I might not exist at all. And so in many ways, my life is owed to our lack of money. I grew up watching my parents, and particularly my mother, toil for every scrap we ate. So often they would fill the plates of my sister and I and claim they weren't hungry. They demonstrated that hard work was the only route to survival. This gave me the incentive to prove to the world and, especially, to my mother that I could become whatever I wanted. How could I not be inspired by the many sacrifices she had made for her children?

My adult life has not been a struggle for survival and it's important to note the distinction here between living and existing. It is my greatest desire that my family and I are able not just to eat and maintain a home but also to thrive, to enjoy things, to travel and visit places of culture, to read books that we have bought and give our children toys to play with. Living is the part that comes after existing. And as children, my sister and I were forced to deal much more with the everyday strain of the latter than the former.

The last thing I want, having worked hard and ethically

all my life, is to sit on money when it's so desperately needed elsewhere. I'd like to become more involved with charities in China to help poor children and provide them with food and education. I know what it is like to pick the last scraps of meat off chicken bones or wander the streets looking for discarded sugar canes. If I am able to help just one family lift themselves out of poverty I will be happy. I'd also like to have a family myself now that I have built up a stable business, which gives me time to enjoy family life.

I have three stories which I would like to share and I decided to leave them until this last chapter. They all concern people I have already mentioned.

The first is about Alan Bennett, the owner of Davies & Son in Savile Row. In 2007 he asked me if I could source some high-quality handmade ties with unique designs. I managed to find a factory in China which produced ties, mainly for Italian companies, who agreed to run up a few samples. Alan was impressed with the ties and asked me how much I would charge. I replied that they would be six pounds per tie but the minimum order had to be 50 ties per pattern. "Biao, you are only charging me six pounds a tie but for this quality, you should charge at least twelve pounds." He explained that he wanted a long-term partnership where both of our companies made a reasonable profit. I took this as a sign of support from Alan for my work. He took me under his wing, at his own expense, to mentor me in the world of men's bespoke tailoring. He came with me to China on quite a few occasions and in fact trained my workshop tailors whilst there. To this day, his kindness towards me continues and we are still firm friends – I learnt so much from him that has enabled me to be successful with my own tailoring businesses.

The second story is about Bryon. He was taken to the Accident and Emergency Department at the Luton & Dunstable University Hospital in August 2019. He had fainted at home due to severe arrhythmia. He required emergency treatment to stabilise his heart beat and was subsequently transferred to the Coronary Care Unit (CCU) where he stayed for eleven days. The care and attention Bryon received on that ward was exceptional. Each day I went to visit him, the staff dedication was really evident to me. I would spend most days at Bryon's bedside to keep him company during his recovery. A couple of days before his release we spoke about how we could show our appreciation. In order to comply with the hospital charity rules, we sought donations from business contacts and friends so that the hospital could purchase equipment for sole CCU use and pay for additional training for the nurses on the ward. We were both extremely pleased to present £4,500 to the Ward Sister in November and the story appeared on the local press.

My friendship with Bryon taught me a great deal, not only about business, but also about life itself. Bryon had a very caring nature and, all through our long friendship, he remained a role model for me. We meet people as we journey through life who are special and Bryon is top of my list. His generous support for charities has been passed on to me and, even when he was ill towards the end of his life, he always wanted to know how I was doing. Why did I want to share this with you now? Embrace and cherish the special people you meet on your journey through life. They are priceless beyond words.

The last of the three stories is saved for my mum. One day in 2008, the living room was cosy and warm, with the television glowing in the corner. My mum, sitting on the sofa, clicked the remote and stumbled upon a news story that caught her attention. It was a report from Hangzhou, featuring an elderly woman named Mrs. Xie, who had fainted on the street and ended up in the City hospital. The television showed images of her lying in the hospital bed, all alone.

The news anchor's voice was full of concern, saying that Mrs. Xie had nobody visiting her to help with meals or medication bills. My mum looked at my stepfather and said, "My conscience is telling me we have to help her. Can you imagine being in her place?"

My stepfather nodded, understanding the gravity of the situation, and the next day, my mum prepared a wholesome meal and took a bus to the hospital. When she walked into Mrs. Xie's room, the atmosphere changed instantly. Mrs. Xie couldn't believe her eyes; she was visibly moved that a stranger had taken such trouble for her.

"I lost my husband a few years ago and my daughter is in Australia. I didn't want to worry her," Mrs. Xie explained, her eyes misty.

"I completely understand," my mum said, touching Mrs. Xie's arm gently. "I would do the same if I were in your shoes."

That day, my mum also paid Mrs. Xie's hospital bill, ensuring she could receive further treatment. For the next four weeks, either my mum or stepfather would bring food to Mrs. Xie daily, brightening her room with their presence and love.

Mrs. Xie was touched beyond words and began to see them as her own family. The friendship between her and my parents deepened, and they became a regular part of each other's lives.

Soon enough, the TV station caught wind of this extraordinary act of kindness and came to interview my mum. The reporter asked her, "Why are you doing this for Mrs. Xie?"

Looking into the camera, my mum said, "I have a son who is also abroad. Just like Mrs. Xie, I wouldn't want to worry him about what's happening back home. Sometimes, helping a stranger is like helping a part of your own family."

The room fell silent for a moment, touched by her sincerity. And that's how my mum not only changed the life of Mrs. Xie but also taught everyone a profound lesson about the beauty of human kindness.

I have been richly blessed to have this kind and generous woman as my mum. The story above captures so much about how she puts others first – putting me and my education first was her priority and for that I am deeply indebted to her. We grow and develop through those we encounter in our lives and our experiences shape who we are and become. My mum's values are embedded into my life now and I try every day to live up to them with those I know and work with.

It remains one of the great inequalities of the world that some children are born light years ahead of others.

They may come from more stable homes, from wealthy homes, from homes with cleaners and domestic staff, cooks and tutors. Everything is easier, more streamlined, more conducive to educational and career success. Others will come from one-bedroom huts with no running water and no electricity, little chance of a good education, and little time to do anything besides work. The child born into a rich family will, no doubt, progress at a faster rate and develop the sort of self-assurance that comes from stability. This is the case wherever you're from; it is as true of communist societies as it is of capitalist ones. I have travelled the world and seen these inequalities. I have witnessed the problems such different starting blocks can bring. But if I've learned anything, it is that success is possible, whatever your situation and however your life begins.

Looking back, it's clear that my greatest wealth was never in material possessions, but in the richness of experience, in relationships and in the indomitable spirit to strive – a life lived in line with Seneca's wisdom that 'the greatest wealth is a poverty of desires.'

As I pen the closing words of this chapter and, indeed, of my autobiography, I can't help but echo Barry Draper's sentiment: "But the road doesn't end here." My life's story is a work in progress, as is yours. I've faced ups and downs, struggles and triumphs, all of which have shaped me into the person I am today. While I find myself in a fortunate position now, being a self-made multi-millionaire, it's vital to remember that there's much more to be done. I aspire to make an impact, no matter how small, in rectifying the global imbalances that I've personally encountered. I want to empower those less fortunate, particularly children who face challenges similar to those I once faced.

I carry with me the wisdom imparted by remarkable people who have crossed my path – Alan Bennett, who schooled me in the importance of equitable business practices; Bryon Sawyer, a role model who impressed upon me the utmost value of compassion and friendship; and above all, my mother and sister, the epitome of selfless love and sacrifice. They serve as my guiding stars as I venture further, especially into the realm of charity.

I dream of a day when a child in a tiny village in China, or indeed any corner of the world, will not have to fret about their next meal, or where their next pair of shoes will come from, or whether they'll have access to quality education. If my story can inspire even one person to overcome obstacles, to strive for better, then I will consider my life's journey a meaningful one.

Life is an ongoing process, an endless series of choices and opportunities. So, let this not be an end, but rather a milestone. If a small poor boy fishing for prawns on a lake in Ningbo can make it this far, then believe me, so can you. Here's to our collective journey ahead, filled with endless possibilities and immeasurable potential.

Thank you for sharing in my story. Now, it's time for you to write your own.

JOURNEY TO THE WEST

Bryon and I presented £4,500 to the Ward Sister in October 2019

ACKNOWLEDGEMENT

Penning this book presented both a linguistic and emotional challenge for me. Navigating the intricate nuances of English, a language foreign to my native tongue, while grappling with the introspective journey of recounting my life's episodes was no small feat. In Chinese culture, we often wear a stoic mask, veiling our true emotions. My gratitude is immeasurable towards Jeffrey Taylor, a revered film producer from both Los Angeles and London, for incessantly pushing me out of my comfort zone. His nudges towards transparency and candour in my narrative were invaluable.

I feel deeply grateful for Barry Draper (1950 – 2023) and Bryon Sawyer (1937 – 2019). Since we first met in 2002 and 2003, their consistent support and friendship have been like a guiding light for me. Their faith in my potential was the vital trigger that encouraged me to start my writing journey in 2020.

A heartfelt thank you to Carol Huxley, Roger Green, Philip Jones, Jez Wilcox, and John Davidson for their meticulous editing, ensuring every word resonated with clarity and intent. To those who painstakingly combed through the drafts, your feedback was the compass guiding this ship: Bernie Raffe, Barry Draper, Francis Perry, Brian Edwards, Rosemary Gadsby, Jenny Shi, Andrew and Sue Livingston, Stella Gill and Chris Canfield. Additionally, a special nod to Jonathan Bodsworth for his exceptional work with illustrations and image edits.

The bedrock of my journey, my unwavering pillars of strength, are my phenomenal mother and my fiercely loving sister. Their sacrifices, love, and faith in me have been the driving force behind every step I've taken. They, alongside my close-knit family, are the unsung heroines and heroes of my tale.

The past six months, dedicated to writing my life's story, have been a profound period of self-reflection. It's my ardent wish that my chronicle serves as a beacon of hope and inspiration to every reader.

Biao Wang
Leighton Buzzard, Bedfordshire
September 2023

ABOUT THE AUTHOR

Biao Wang

From the humble beginnings of an impoverished rural village in China to the bustling streets of the UK, Biao's story is not just a testament to the human spirit but also a guidebook on the power of perseverance, vision, and the strength that arises from a challenging backdrop. His tale is a beacon, illuminating what one can achieve with grit and imagination, irrespective of one's starting point in life.

Charting his own course was never an option for Biao; it was a necessity. His ambition carried him far from the familiar terrains of his remote farming roots. Yet, even as he soared to new heights, the tapestry of his journey was always stitched with gratitude. He constantly remembered the individuals who lent him a hand, guiding him through uncharted territories, especially during his transition to the enigmatic realm of England.

Writing this memoir has allowed Biao to unfurl his treasure trove of experiences. His candid recounting of building a global career is sprinkled with humour, introspection, and touching moments of human connection. Whether it's a jovial anecdote about understanding cultural nuances or heartening tales of forging bonds in unfamiliar territories, his stories resonate deeply, offering both laughter and reflection.

Life is a mosaic of varied experiences, and Biao revels in the exploration of novel thoughts and ideas. Whether he's conversing in Mandarin or English, communication remains his bridge to understanding and connection. His two-decade-long sojourn in the UK has been an eye-opener; while societal structures appeared distinct initially, with time he recognised the universality of human experiences. The amusing realisation that the Cockney slang 'My Old China' translates to 'my old mate' is just one of many delightful discoveries he encountered.

At the core, Biao's journey underscores the magic that unfolds when unwavering dedication meets the support of genuine friendships and familial love. His aspirations extend beyond personal triumphs; he passionately believes in elevating others alongside him. Through his narrative, he hopes to inspire, emphasising the paramount importance of sharing successes and lifting others as you rise.

Printed in Poland
by Amazon Fulfillment
Poland Sp. z o.o., Wrocław